Homeschooling All the Way
through High School

Home-
schooling
All the Way
through
High
School

RENEE MASON

TYNDALE HOUSE PUBLISHERS, INC.
WHEATON, ILLINOIS

Visit Tyndale's exciting Web site at www.tyndale.com

Unless otherwise indicated, all Scripture quotations are taken from the *Holy Bible*, New International Version®. NIV®. Copyright © 1973, 1978, 1984, by International Bible Society. Used by permission of Zondervan Publishing House. All rights reserved.

Scripture quotations marked KJV are taken from the *Holy Bible*, King James Version.

First edition 1999

Library of Congress Cataloging-in-Publication Data

Mason, Renee.
   Homeschooling all the way through high school / Renee Mason.
     p. cm.
   ISBN 0-8423-3449-1
1. Home schooling. I. Title.
LC40.M37 1999
371.04'2—dc21   99-32337

Printed in the United States of America

04 03 02 01 00 99

7 6 5 4 3 2

Contents

Introduction

This book was written in the midst of schooling seven of our of eight children. Eight children! Yes, praise their creator—eight. The oldest has been busy this past year earning her college degree and beginning law school. While completing her senior year, she contributed to this manuscript with great insight. The next two daughters contributed as part of their schoolwork. Each contribution to this book reveals the character and dimension of a large family's learning to submit to the path God has chosen for it.

While most of our family was attending Bill Gothard's Institute in Basic Life Principles during the summer of 1996, I was driving around the seminar area in Orlando, entertaining my busy one- and three-year-olds. My five-, ten-, and eight-year-olds were attending the children's seminar and my fourteen-year-old was at the adult seminar with Dad. The sixteen-year-old was on a summer mission trip, and the twenty-one-year-old was working at her summer job back home in Ft. Lauderdale. It takes strategy to manage a family of this size.

I was only able to attend the last thirty minutes of the final session on the last day of the seminar. Bill Gothard was there in person, rather than on tape. You could feel the Holy Spirit's presence. There was an excitement generated among the crowd as we heard spiritual principles and truths explained from God's Word. Bill quoted a Scripture that hit me like a brick: "In all thy ways acknowledge him, and he shall direct thy paths" (Proverbs 3:6 KJV). I realized I was being spoken to by my Savior. I asked God then and there how I was to acknowledge him, at which point my husband turned to me and said, "You should write a book and share your experiences in homeschooling. Others would benefit from our blessing."

The first question I asked was, "How?" Almost immediately Norm Wise's name came to mind. I knew I must contact Norm. He had been an elder at the church we had attended for seventeen years. I knew Norm was working for Coral Ridge Ministries, but I was not sure in what capacity. After some time I finally called for an appointment, and he replied that he would be glad to advise me. The day arrived and I went excitedly to the main facility of Coral Ridge, but I had failed to ask Norm exactly where on the campus his office was located. After walking no more than ten feet, I saw his wife Terry. She just happened to be there. (Or was it the providence of God, leading me in his gracious way?)

My oldest daughter, Donielle, had come along with me; I think I brought her to be a second set of ears. If I missed something important, she would remember. As we entered Norm's office, I noticed boxes lining the walls. I asked Norm what they were for.

"This is my last day at Coral Ridge Ministries," he replied.

I could not believe what I had heard! I had procrastinated the bidding of God until the last moment. Step by step Norm showed us the basics of writing a book.

I could share other instances of how God has led in the writing of this book. Although *Homeschooling All the Way through High School* will receive neither Nobel nor Pulitzer prizes, God, the great creator of all things, who upholds, directs, and governs those he has called, in the greatest and the least of circumstances, has asked me to acknowledge him in our family and school, and I will obey. These stories have been written in the midst of homeschooling, church activities, organizing the harvest festival, nursing the baby, teaching a six-year-old to read, preparing our eighteen-year-old to graduate, cleaning the house, and feeding the cat. My heart overflows as I see my eight children, hear my husband read the Bible after the noon meal, and look out at the meandering New River on which our seventy-five-year-old house is located. I see his fingerprints on our lives as we see the infinite goodness of God.

How to Read this Book

As you read this book, you will see inserts written by the author's children. Donielle, twenty-three, completed homeschool high school (complete with graduation ceremony), and went on to finish college. If you are now homeschooling your children, you will freshen your commitment to homeschool as you read this young lady's wisdom and insight gained from years spent at home nurturing her character.

Donna, nineteen, will add her views as an upcoming high school graduate from homeschool. She shares her inspirations as she grows up and enters adulthood and tells how homeschool has helped her develop spiritually.

Danee, sixteen, explains her freedom to be creative and how she has grown in every area of her life as a result of the flexibility gained through homeschooling. She stresses family bonding.

Frank, ten, tells in his childlike way, how he has grown because of the responsibilities given to him and expectations that the jobs would be well done.

Grammy (Ginny Douglas) challenges grandparents to experience the rewards of being involved in grandchildren's education while assisting the parents in teaching.

Dad (Frank) will share some projects you can do in your homeschool.

All of the inserts are headed with the name of the writer. The rest of the book is written by the homeschooling mom, Renee Mason. She shares her experience in homeschooling eight children for fourteen years to encourage and challenge those who are homeschooling or are considering it. Throughout this book you will see what drives this family—a constant determination to please the founder of their school, Jesus Christ!

1

Getting Started

It was over thirteen years ago that God put it on my heart to homeschool my children. At the time Donielle, our oldest, had almost completed fifth grade at a nearby Christian school. It was a good school for the most part, and we tried to stay involved as much as we could. The headmaster and his wife were good friends of ours. We would often get into lengthy discussions about what Christian schools and the responsibilities of Christian parents should be.

It was on a warm spring afternoon, when I was picking up my daughter from school, that God began to point the way down the road he wished us to travel.

Oh no, I thought—here they come again. Walking toward me was a couple from church that I had been trying to avoid recently. They had these big, self-assured grins on their faces and they were coming straight toward me. Their arms were always around each other like newlyweds. I thought, *How could two people have such grins on their faces, and be so lovey-dovey at 2:01 P.M. in this place?* It seemed like hundreds of kids were running and screaming as the bell rang. Outside the temperature was around ninety degrees, and I was in no mood to talk to these know-it-all people. I tried to figure out how to avoid them graciously, but how could I hide? It seemed like all of their conversations these days were about homeschooling. I wondered how these people could teach their children at home—all four of them! How could they afford it? I knew their kind, and I did not want to be like them, so I tried to slip by without their noticing me. It was too late. With no exit at the opposite end of the hall, I was trapped.

As a group of children passed by, bumping me on the way, I was relieved to see a classmate of Donielle's, a boy named Alfred who had spent many weeks at our home as a guest. He had become our oldest daughter's best friend. He had always defended her and she him. I called out and asked how he was. I will never forget the look on his downcast face as he answered, "Not so good, Mrs. Mason." I had grown to love this boy and recognized that he was very troubled. I asked him what the problem was. With his eyes still on the ground he told me, "All the guys in the class are making fun of me. I don't belong here." The only black student in the school, Alfred was a special young man with a unique set of problems. We discovered later that his mother had a terminal illness and one of his brothers had recently died of AIDS. Another case of innocent children, trying to survive in a world built around their peers.

I gave Alfred a quick hug and started back down the hall. The friends that I had been trying to avoid were now face-to-face with me. My stomach sank to my feet as Blake said to me, "Renee, Shari and I have been wanting to come over and talk to you and Frank. When is a good time?" I did not want to talk to them. I already knew what their mission was. I had heard enough of their well-thought-out sermon which I thought should be titled "Maybe God Wants You to Homeschool Your Children." The pastor of our church also homeschooled, but he had never tried to convert us to his way of thinking. He seemed to have a more toned-down, quiet way of homeschooling. When I thought about it, there was something different, maybe special about the behavior and personalities of his two children. They seemed obedient and respectful, different than the children with whom my daughter went to school.

As I thought about our busy schedule, I honestly could not think of a time when my husband and I were free. Besides working as janitors here at our daughter's school to defray tuition, we were also janitors at another school to pay the remainder of the tuition. And in the daytime I held a position as a school crossing guard. Between three part-time jobs and being a mom to three little girls, I was tired. My husband had his full-time job in addition to helping me with the janitorial work. Then there were all the side jobs he did just to make ends meet. It took lots of hard work just to be able to afford a Christian school for my daughters.

Donielle had spent first grade in a public school, but our convictions were that our children must have a Christ-centered education. This was her last year at this school because it only went up to fifth grade. We had been checking into other Christian schools, doing our homework. Even though it had been a decent school, we were not pleased with several of her teachers. Maybe we were just too picky—or were the teachers, in fact, not meeting the standards we felt were crucial for a Christian school? These were issues with which my husband and I had been struggling. I looked at Blake and Shari and said, "Just call us and we'll make the time to talk with you." As Blake looked at me and saw the questions in my eyes, he reached out and patted my shoulder. At that moment I saw a caring man, a man who was concerned about the future of his children as well as others. I thought, *This man would make a good minister.* Many years have passed, and the mark Blake and Shari Burnside left on our lives will never be forgotten. Now Blake is a full-time minister with a congregation of his own.

As I finished my conversation with them I had many doubts about the possibility of starting our own homeschool. I wondered how I could take on such a task. How could I find the time? Ideas and questions were racing through my mind as I headed to my car to go home. I had a sick feeling at the bottom of my stomach that I only experience when making a major decision in my life. Between that sick feeling and the heat of the afternoon, all I wanted was to get the air-conditioning going in the car. I buckled my kids in their seats and turned on the radio. I wanted to distract myself from all of these thoughts about homeschooling. But, for whatever the reason, I turned to the right station. I had listened no more than a minute when the announcer said there would be a homeschool conference at what was then Miami Christian College. The lead speakers would be Dr. Raymond and Dorothy Moore. Blake had mentioned their books and had even asked me to read one, *Home Grown Kids.* Well, I had heard enough! I quickly tuned in the other Christian radio station to which I often listened. I could not believe my ears—this station was playing the same commercial! Was this a coincidence, or was I supposed to hear this commercial? I decided to pay attention. Maybe my husband and I should attend the conference. I felt the hair on my arms rise. Were all these homeschooling conversations I had had with the Burnsides lately part of a larger plan? I could not help but think maybe we were supposed to homeschool.

I knew the next step would be to talk to my overworked husband. I needed his counsel. Frank has a practical way of looking at things. When I arrived home, he was on the phone. I announced, "Frank, when you are off the phone we need to talk." He gave me a look that said, "What about?" He sensed my urgency and quickly ended his conversation.

I told him about my conversation with Blake and Shari, not looking forward to the reaction I thought I would receive. When I told him about the upcoming seminar, I never imagined he would give the response he did, due to our busy schedules: "Yes, let's plan on going."

I was starting to get excited. It was one thing to consider taking on this task myself, but if I had known I would have the help and cooperation of my husband, what we would soon face, we would face together, praise God!

Danielle

On that drive home I listened to the homeschool seminar ads with interest that equaled my mother's. It sounded like a great idea to me. I had always been close to my mother. She had taught me to read and write before I ever went to school. I was unhappy with my teachers. The only time I was truly happy in school was in music and drama classes once a week. So when my mom suddenly asked me, "Do you think you would like to homeschool?" I immediately answered with an enthusiastic yes.

It seems that was the final straw on her pile of frustration. As I sat with wide eyes in the passenger seat she began a tirade of excuses in my general direction. "But I can't! What would my family think? My parents would criticize—and my brothers! They would definitely make fun of me. And your father's parents, they are public-school teachers!"

This monologue lasted until we got out of the car. Occasionally I glanced towards the backseat where my sister Donna, then a kindergartner, looked back at me and shrugged. Three-year-old Danee giggled. All three of us were relieved to get out of the car, not sure what had just happened. What makes this incident so hilarious to me now is that both of my mom's brothers began homeschooling several years later. One of them is homeschooling his sons through high school. My cousin, Brian, and my sister, Donna both graduated from homeschool high school last spring! □

The seminar went all too quickly. In the Lord's usual style of teaching me, before the day was out my head was stuffed with ideas. I felt that before the seminar was over I just had to speak with Dr. Moore. For some reason I felt the need to speak with him personally. After waiting in line for quite some time, I saw my opening. Then someone quickly stepped up to Dr. Moore and I realized I had missed my opportunity. I felt such disappointment that such a discourteous person had probably caused me to miss my chance, since the next session would begin soon, and the personal question time was coming to a close. I dropped my head, feeling discouraged. I probably would not get another chance, and I felt such a need to discuss my daughters with him. My husband suddenly motioned for me to look up. As I did I saw Dr. Moore standing in front of me! I was so thankful. I began telling him about my daughters and the schooling they had received. As I finished, I looked forward to what words of wisdom Dr. Moore would bestow. He began to relate his own experience, and I felt that he had heard my story a million times before. He spoke such encouragement and left me with the feeling that I could do it. I could educate my children at home!

When I left him, my head was swimming and I felt like I would burst. I remember our ride home that day. I knew our decision to homeschool was the right one, and I felt such joy. I also felt like an athlete ready to dive off the high dive. It was like relinquishing our will to do God's plan—it is the right thing to do, and God's will is right for our lives. We had the remainder of the school year and the summer before we would begin our homeschool. So much to do, so much to prepare.

I questioned even where to begin. With that question a feeling of calm came over me, and it became clear where to begin. Begin with prayer. In God's Word we are told, "Very early in the morning, while it was still dark, Jesus got up, left the house and went off to a solitary place, where he prayed" (Mark 1:35). I felt the need, now more than ever, to seek God's direction. So my first two steps were to commit all of this to prayer, and to join the Broward County homeschool parent support group. I asked so many questions of the ladies who directed the group that I am sure God must have given them an extra measure of patience.

As I prepared for school the next year, I researched various curricula. Some of the many benefits of belonging to a support group are the curriculum fairs and shares. Many sell and buy books and other supplies through our support group. We have been blessed to have a grandmother who is a teacher in the public school system, who helps us in our curriculum choice.

I was on my way in preparing for that first day of school at "Riverview Academy." We chose that name because we lived on the New River. We also wanted to name our school so when people asked our daughters where they went to school, they could tell them and maybe avoid some eyebrow raising. Most people had no idea what homeschooling was anyway. What we did not bargain for was the next question—where was it located? My oldest daughter would proudly answer, "At home!" Eyebrows were raised even higher. I will never forget the time a person asked my daughter where she went to school, and she told them Riverview Academy. The person answered, "Oh yes. I know where that is." That time I raised *my* eyebrows.

Once a friend of mine was in the supermarket with her four children during the school day when an older woman very curtly asked why her children were not in the nearby public school. My friend politely answered that they were in school. She explained that menu planning, using coupons, and selecting fruits and vegetables for a dish they were planning were all part of their curriculum. The woman left, obviously unconvinced about the merits of homeschooling. One of the biggest challenges is in examining the way education should be. We have been trained to think it is normal and good to send that tiny little one away on the bus, in new clothes, with a new lunch box, and maybe with a bright red apple to get on the good side of the teacher. While that little one screams and cries and our heart breaks, we question if maybe we should have kept the child home. Maybe we should have! And as the bus drives away we see that precious face pressed against the school-bus window with a look that says, "Why, Mom, why?" Maybe we should ponder all of this and realize there are other ways of nurturing, ways that are better for all. Our society, unfortunately, has set an example which we are taught to believe we should follow. I am not saying that all of what society has to offer is bad; there is, in fact, some good in its ideas. But what I am saying is that, in God's plan, there is more than one way to get the job done.

I was excited and happy. I was happy to have my oldest home all day. People have questioned how I could stand having my children around me all day without a break. Actually, Donielle was a great help with her little sisters. All of the nonacademic projects that we did together, like baking and arts and crafts, bonded us. We were always getting to know each other better. I enjoyed teaching my children to cook, and the measuring and doubling of recipes taught them to work with fractions. As the school year progressed we not only made gifts for Christmas, but we also performed plays and skits and wrote stories and poems using spelling words.

Danielle

We began homeschooling when I entered sixth grade. We converted the front room of our house into a schoolroom. Our bulletin boards were big ceiling tiles glued to the walls. There was a desk for each of us, and an air conditioner that you had to shout over to ask a question. But it was an exciting place—not a place made for education, but a place where education was made real. I spent the last of my grade school days learning there. Not only in that room, however! I have homeschooling memories in every room of our house—and beyond! That is the beauty of homeschooling; there is no limit to the possibilities. Many people asked me back in those days, "What is going to happen when you get out into the real world?" Homeschooling *is* education in the real world! It is the opposite of sequestering students between four walls with only their peers as influences, where they cannot learn to relate to adults. It is hands-on, internship-to-adulthood learning.   □

As time went on, some of our relatives began to challenge me. An aunt sent a letter asking us to please realize that we were not trained teachers and were incapable of giving our daughter the education so essential to women today, where women must achieve in a man's world. A grandfather sent a letter with a newspaper article about a backwoods family in Kentucky who kept their children at home. The article mentioned that the children's language consisted of babble. I suppose he felt this was homeschooling. Because we remained steadfast in our convictions and continued to homeschool despite his reservations, he eventually broke all ties with us. The consolation we have found has come from Jesus, who never promised we would be loved for following the plans he has made for us. We were feeling the pains of walking close to him.

I remember times when I doubted if I could go any further as Donielle's subjects became more complicated, and I remember becoming impatient with her progress. By the end of year one I wondered if she had learned anything, especially when she took year-end tests required by the State of Florida. (Our support group provides this testing service to its members.) All of the parents felt as if they were being tested, too. I was always thankful when excellent results came back.

Donielle loves to read, as all of our children do. At the end of the day, when she would share historical facts she had read (facts I had never learned), I learned to listen. When I began to doubt myself, or her, I would listen. I would hear her read to her little sisters, or share something new and profound she had read that day. This was all so new to me. My impatience only made me nervous. I am sure there were days when I was hard to live with, and I regret those days. Donielle's name should have been Grace. She was so gracious in those early days of homeschooling. I could always see God's grace in her. She was kind and patient with me and my expectations. She was glad to be home with me. I was her teacher and she respected me as such. My children have always had a God-given respect for me, something many children lack today. She cooperated and did her lessons as she was told. There is a family down the river from us who homeschooled their boys. They always put it this way: the boys look at their mom not as a chauffeur, laundress, cook, or maid. They look at her as the one who has taught them everything they know. I call it "total mothering."

Danee

Because I have been homeschooled all of my life, I have focused on the needs of my family and the things that draw us closer. In our house we love to celebrate birthdays, holidays, and other special occasions. We bake, decorate, sing, and do all sorts of other things.

I think it is very special to have the whole family participate in holiday activities as part of our school. When I say "holiday activity," I do not mean only Christmas, but all of the holidays, like Valentine's Day, Easter, Thanksgiving, and others. Psalm 133:1 says, "How good and pleasant it is when brothers live together in unity." Holiday activities, which soon become traditions, are important in the unity of a homeschool and of a family. Families should not be just a group of related people, they should be a group of people who love each other enough to spend time doing things together.

One thing I find in our family, which I think comes from homeschooling, is unity. All of my brothers and sisters learn from each other. As a helper in our homeschool and a member of our family, I like to work on finding the interests and talents of each person in our family, making sure no one gets left out or feels less special. Then we turn those interests into action in ways that will be fun, and most importantly, ways that will give God the glory—what we were created for! We do not always do these things during school hours. They can be done any time of the day or year, but for us they are school. Homeschool is life in general: learning from your family while they learn from you, and everyone contributes. My brothers and sisters learn more from hands-on activities than from book work.

Our family memories are so important because they stay with us as we grow older. Without memories our past would be blank. When we think back to our childhood, we think of special memories with our family. When we have our own children, we will use these memories to create memories for them. I remember one fall day when my sister Ameleigh kept asking, "Can I help?"

"I guess you can," Mom finally answered, "but wash your hands." Soon the echo came, first from my brothers, then my other sisters.

"I want to mix the batter," Daniel said.

"I can't reach and Darleen won't let go of my chair," Diana complained.

"How high can I turn the oven?" Frank hollered.

Above all the ruckus, my mother patiently told each of them what to do and how to do it. After cleaning all the sugar off the counters, the flour out of the cabinets, and the sticky batter off the floor, a delicious batch of cookies had been made. Each person was able to say that he had had a part in making the cookies. Without realizing it, they had made a memory that would last forever. Now I will admit, we do not always have the time or energy to spend baking cookies and cleaning up messes. Sometimes I would just rather do it all myself, and that is perfectly fine. Remember though, that extra half hour spent with your family will turn into lifelong memories for them. It is worth the investment.

2

Using Grandparents and
Other Resources

My mother has been very helpful throughout our years of homeschooling. She has come over once a week to hold language and writing classes. My mom has always wanted to be a writer. She has written many beautiful poems and essays through the years. Everyone looks forward to her traditional Christmas poem each year. She loves life, and it spills over to her grandchildren; she loves to mother them. Whether it is with peach cobbler when peaches are in season or fudge at Christmastime, each child is made to feel important by Grammy. In our second year of homeschooling we began to have classes with Grammy. They have been great! For the few hours that she teaches each week I can catch up on the laundry or even relax with a glass of iced tea! And it is wonderful to see Granddad come into the picture now. An ardent builder, he comes over and teaches the boys, ages ten and twelve, about nails and measuring. He recently went over the multiplication tables with them. They learned quickly when they found out that Granddad would be doing the testing! Lately the youngest girls, ages seven, five, and three, have decided they are going to be Granddad's teacher, instructing him in music. He passed country and western, but he flunked rock 'n' roll. As our family grew, Grammy and Granddad never missed an event. I can never forget all of the loose teeth he pulled and all of the tales he told to go along with them.

Grammy

I admire parents so dedicated to their children that they take on the responsibility of homeschooling. I feel it is my duty to help. The following list shows some of the ways in which I help.

• I teach classes once a week in my children's homes.

• I teach them to write stories, poems, essays, and all forms of journalism. We have also put together our own newsletter. We call it *Grammy's Home Journal*.

• I often take them places for field trips.

• I baby-sit so their parents can get out once in a while.

• I make the best peach cobbler and the yummiest fudge at Christmastime.

One observation I have made is that homeschoolers have a deep love and respect for God. I often feel sorry for the burden mothers carry in their dedication to home-school. I pay tribute to homeschooling mothers every-where for their unselfish love and devotion. Speaking as a mother, we have made many mistakes, I am sure; but for the most part, a mother takes her role seriously and loves with an enduring heart.

It is important to leave your grandchildren with good memories during these formative years. I will give you a glimpse of my mother's impact on my life. Mother was patient, wise, and understanding. Her life fit Proverbs 31:10-31 quite well. I can still smell the scent of fresh loaves of bread that she would bake on a summer's day. How mouth-watering! After my brothers and I had come from swimming in the picturesque stream that meandered by our home, she would have warm bread ready for us. Today I can still recall the enticing aroma of the fruits and vegetables she used to prepare in our kitchen for winter use. This canning went on all summer long and into the fall.

A great deal has been written about mothers. Through the years I have talked with many of them. I have never met one yet that did not love her children with a sacrificial love that was unbelievable. To be a good mother nowadays one must have the brains of Einstein, the strength of Hercules, the patience of Job, and the humor of Bob Hope. She must also be a nursemaid, cook, cleaning lady, gardener, chauffeur, lawyer, teacher, and above all, an angel. One must know how to say yes and no, stop and go. Is it any wonder that Lincoln said, "All I am and ever hope to be, I owe to my angel mother!"

I cannot understand for the life of me how my mother survived my teen years. I topped them all! I would take an hour to dress, then would wail, "I am so ugly! I can't wear this awful dress." Then back to the bedroom I would go for another half hour or so. My grandma used to complain that

I had to have every hair on my head in place before I left the house. I think that is how I acquired my habit of being late for Sunday school.

It is a long, hard haul to reach the top. When we see the last child walk down the aisle we should be relieved and say, "Thank you, God!" But no, not us. We moan and groan and wail and say "It seems like only yesterday they were so tiny. I miss them already." I know I could write an exciting book about parenthood that would take a lifetime to read. It would be entitled *My Life As a Mother*. I would start with my firstborn, and go through the growing years all the way to becoming a grandma. Isn't parenthood exciting? We never know what to expect next. Now take being a grandmother—it is such a beautiful and rewarding time with those darling little ones. Our love feels unsurpassable. And we only have to take care of them when we want to. Isn't that great?

All jokes aside, it is important to honor and encourage mothers. Grandparents can fill that job well. Parents today have such a difficult and tiring responsibility. With alcohol, drugs, and premarital sex so commonplace, it is easy to understand why there is such a high abortion rate. We must pray for our children who have young adult children, that God gives them great gifts so that they know how to teach their children to desire a life dedicated to God.

Being a parent is a great gift. No gift can be lovelier. Homeschooling is a wonderful way to use that gift. It is so rewarding when we bring them to adulthood and know we tried to do our very best. What better gift can we give our grandchildren than ourselves?

At Christmastime I thought about what gifts I should give my grandchildren and wrote this poem.

What Will I Give Them?

Everything was chaotic as could be!
Christmas was coming in a hurry.
My head was splitting with too much worry.
What will I give them?
My seventeen grandchildren, who else?
Just then something clicked in my head.
That still, small voice whispered I had nothing to dread.
"Give of yourself," it softly said.
First and foremost give them faith, hope and charity, mixed
*   with love of God and mankind.*
Give your attention, for one day it will be too late.
Give them a sense of humor, the world loves laughter.
Give them kindness to soothe many a heart.
Give them patience for happy living, peaceful and serene.
These are just a few, precious virtues that were given to me,
*   and are not new.*
This is their heritage this Christmas day from their Grammy.
It's not so much that we give, but what we share.

I would encourage grandparents everywhere to take an active part in the schooling of their grandchildren. Dig around in your mind for a special skill or talent you can share. Teach them about their family history. Or just offer your services and see where you are needed. Your children will appreciate your support. The rewards are eternal. I have been so blessed by my involvement in my grandchildren's homeschool.   □

Since we began to homeschool fourteen years ago our family has grown from three girls to six girls and two boys, eight in all. All but three were born in the comfort of our home with midwives present.

Danee

Mother feels that it is not natural to have a baby in the hospital. Hospitals are for sick people. What a way to spend your birthday—in the hospital! I think it makes sense to have a baby at home. One of the most awesome home-school classes I have had is to watch and participate in the birth of my five younger siblings. Four were born at home, and one in a birthing center.

Mom was due to have Darleen any day. It was August 16, about 7:30 in the morning. She was on the job checking crossing guards. My sister Donna was with her. Mom said her contractions were getting closer together and she needed to stop and get something to drink. When they pulled into a McDonald's parking lot and bought some iced tea, they saw Mom's supervisor. She joked about how Mom sticks to the job until the last minute. Sure enough, she did. She went home and Darleen was born at 3:30 that afternoon. I rubbed her back, got her drinks, and prayed. My sister Donna says that when she gives birth, she just wants the baby to appear magically, or she would be glad to let her husband have the labor pains. After the birth I decorated Darleen's very first birthday cake which my mother made while in labor. □

I have always said school at home does not confine your classroom to four walls with fluorescent lights. You have the world at your fingertips. I once presented a unit study on money with the children. I found a numismatist here in our city who was happy to explain the history of money as we know it. When we did a unit study on oceanography we all boarded our boat and went to Nova

User name: SHAFIEI, SHAHRZAD

Title: Homeschooling all the way through high sc
hool
Author: Mason, Renee.
Item ID: R0091164504
Date due: 5/18/2017,23:59
Current time: 04/20/2017,11:24

Title: Homeschool your child for free
Author: Gold, LauraMaery.
Item ID: R0103478449
Date due: 5/18/2017,23:59
Current time: 04/20/2017,11:24

Title: Absolute beginner's guide to homeschoolin
g
Author: Miser, Brad.
Item ID: R0109489498
Date due: 5/18/2017,23:59
Current time: 04/20/2017,11:24

Title: Georgia milestones grade 8 Mathematics su
ccess st
Author: Mometrix Media LLC.
Item ID: R0170392282
Date due: 5/18/2017,23:59
Current time: 04/20/2017,11:24

University's oceanographic lab near Port Everglades. After the unit study we had a picnic on the beach. Unit studies are an excellent way to give a hands-on, total learning experience. Children never forget such experiences. We have a Museum of Discovery and Science nearby which we use often. When Donna wanted to learn about Florida history, we enrolled her in classes at the Historical Society. She became their youngest docent.

When our older children have trouble with algebra, we have a blessing in Joe. Joe is a retired electrical engineer from Ft. Worth, Texas, who now resides on a sailboat on the river. He has become like an uncle to our family. We have shared many birthdays, holidays, and other family events with him. Joe knows his math! There have been times near end-of-the-year testing when Joe has come over for review classes with our kids.

He is going to do an electricity class this year. The children have a playhouse that they want to wire for electricity. The playhouse was a Christmas gift for all of our children, given about ten years ago. (We often buy one large gift for Christmas that they can all use and enjoy.) All the children enjoyed that playhouse when they were little. Now they think they need electricity in it! They were inspired by an exhibit at the science museum. There was a wiring display, and they showed great interest in the how-to guide. It is rewarding to see them investigate how things work. I also find it rewarding when they plan projects on their own. The students' ability to think for themselves is an accurate measure of your success as a teacher.

We went to a small Presbyterian church for seventeen years. During our time there we had two pastors who homeschooled their children. One of them believed strongly that children should learn the Westminster Shorter Catechism. This catechism sums up important questions in the Bible—I call it a road map through the Bible. He offered catechism classes to homeschoolers in the church. I feel memorization is very important for children, especially Scripture memorization. The Bible instructs us to hide the Word of God in our heart, that we might not sin against him. We always start our day with prayer, Scripture, and catechism memorization. Often parents will share with me that they can hardly get anything done on a school day, or that they are so disorganized. I always encourage them to teach their children to pray and learn Scriptures because these are the most important things. If you have done these, you have done what is most important. In honoring God and putting him first, he will bless you with organization.

Creative teaching and using outside resources greatly enhance your children's education. My husband always says that if the children were attending private or Christian schools, we would be paying plenty. Use some of the money you would have spent on a private education on outside resources. Take some of the money you have saved by homeschooling to hire a tutor if the subject is too much for you to teach. There are also many videos that can supplement your curriculum in any subject. Many older members of your church may be experts in areas you are not and would love to be busy helping you. Neighbors and friends are excellent resources and would love to be asked for help. This is the purpose of a support group, to help one another. You do not have to confine your school to one room—you have the world as a resource. The blessings of being at home with your children can far outweigh the small expense of purchases that will help you do a great job with their education.

Danielle

Several of my friends were fellow homeschool students. Back in those pioneering days for high school homeschoolers, our parent support group decided they needed to divide their field trips, making a separate category for ages eleven and over. My mother volunteered to organize some of these field trips, including visits to the courthouse, (the crime lab there was my favorite), a newspaper, and an executive airport. The educational field trips were the ones I remember most clearly. What could be more educational than being in an airport control tower? Without realizing it, I was being exposed to a myriad of career ideas.

There were some great pool parties at Blake and Shari's house. This gave the middle and high school students a chance to get together to talk and have fun, with lots of planned activities to help break the ice. One such activity was the whipped-cream game. The contestants had to keep their hands behind their backs while they used their mouths to find a gumball in a dish of whipped cream. The first person to find it and blow a bubble won. I always lost. Once while washing the whipped cream off of my face, I met a very sweet girl who was also a ninth grader. We began talking and she asked me if I liked homeschooling. I answered that I did, and asked her the same question.

"I'm trying to talk my mom into letting me go back to school," she told me. "I don't get to be with my friends enough."

At age fourteen homeschooling had already taught me something that most people, including parents and students, seem to have lost sight of, the fact that school is for learning. If you attend a school with all of your friends where the education is less than satisfactory, what are you accomplishing? This subtle form of peer dependency causes some families to put their student back into a traditional school when they reach high school, but they sacrifice the quality of their education. □

Many of the resources available to our children are at the public library. Besides all of the wonderful books, there are audio and videotapes, CDs, computers, periodicals, and more. I thought it would be a great idea to see all that the library has to offer, so we did a unit study on research papers with our teens and some of their friends. After forming an outline on index cards, we went to the library to do some research. Also included in the day's agenda was a tour of the library.

Watching the eyes of my students light up as they worked on the library computers made me value the homeschool day even more, where limited peer involvement can be to our children's advantage. Homeschoolers tend to work well independently. Of course, the student to teacher ratio is not forty to one, but rather one to one. The entire school day is for learning, allowing much more to be accomplished in a shorter amount of time. This allows the schedule to be more flexible for other activities. Because they are not confined for six to eight hours in a building packed with students, they are more serious about the job set before them.

The flexibility of homeschool allows students time for paying jobs. The daughter of a friend who homeschools works three hours a day for a doctor. The doctor is so impressed with her work, he wants to send her to college. Apprenticeship is definitely an option. My nephew Brian, who graduated last spring and is attending Stetson, had his own lawn service. Cottage industries thrive with home-schoolers. Our daughter Danee sells Avon. Donielle, after taking cake-decorating classes as part of her schooling, baked birthday cakes. There are plenty of opportunities for exposure to many vocations.

When we completed our master bedroom I asked the children if they wanted to paint a mural on one of the walls. They all agreed, and we began to research and dream about what the New River looked like before houses were built beside it.

Each of the children contributed to this art class and painted "New River, Unincorporated" on my bedroom wall. The date and all of their signatures are in the corner, except for Darleen whom I was expecting at the time. Even Diana, who was then two years old, contributed. I explained what stippling was and she blobbed the tree tops of the rich Florida oaks. (Of course after she went to bed I helped her contribution some, but she had a great time expressing herself with art.) I have a fascination with lighthouses, and I have involved my children in various murals around our house that depict many of the light-houses I have admired through the years.

We planted a large garden in our yard and the results have been interesting, to say the least. The cherry tomatoes ripened while they were the size of peas, and the broccoli is still not ripe, but the flowers are beautiful, and the children are learning a lot. Our 4-H club, which meets once a month for the entire school day, is a wonderful resource and learning experience for the children, and a tool for socialization in a cooperative environment.

Another wonderful resource for our children's education is the church choir. Music is a vital part of children's education and must not be neglected in their early, formative years. Donielle directed one of the children's choirs last year and sang in the adult choir in her middle and high school years. She took piano lessons as her music education and went on to major in music in college.

We attend the Florida Philharmonic Orchestra children's concert series and other music and theater programs for children whenever we can. A boy down the street attends choir with our children as part of his homeschool. What could be a better outreach than this?

One thing we do in school to prepare for church is to learn sacred hymns. Using the hymnal from church, we learn hymns throughout the school year. We also read about great heroes of the faith, among them, Charles Wesley and John Newton. On Fridays we act out the hymns and sing them, earning points towards the treasure chest. Memorizing Scripture and the Westminster Shorter Catechism also helps the children understand the sermons. It brings them great joy when they know a Scripture text by heart.

Throughout history, singing has characterized God's

people in worship. Singing is an act of worship by which children can praise God, affirm their faith, proclaim spiritual truth, and learn the word of God, and to that end a study in the sacred hymns can nourish and equip them for worship and their education will be more pleasing in the Lord's sight. Hymns can meet the various needs of the people of God, from the simplest informal times among the smallest children, to the most solemn or celebratory occasions in the life of the church. By learning hymns children about God, the church, the Holy Spirit, Jesus Christ, the way of salvation and various aspects of living the Christian life. This training also enables children to take part in adult worship services.

Last year at a high school near our home, an assistant football coach taught our boys weight training. This year our children attended a physical education program sponsored by the Christian Athletic Association. The founder and head coach of this program, Rick Andreassen, is one of the most energetic and inspiring people I know. Coach Rick, as we affectionately and respectfully call him, provides weekly classes at four different parks in our town. The goals of the program are to teach fair play, good sportsmanship, good attitude, and Christian values. He stresses respect to God, parents, leaders, self, one another, equipment, and environment. I would encourage other support groups to promote this type of program. Good physical health requires exercise, and godly instruction promotes godly competition. The theme of his program is "every child is a winner!"

While in Sunday school this past year one of the young men in our fourth- and fifth-grade class began bragging about the soccer team at his school. He was telling how they had won their game the night before. My son Frank joined the conversation by mentioning that he had not played soccer until this year. They all looked at each other with grins on their faces, and the boy telling the soccer-game story began to laugh and make fun of my son exclaiming, "You've never played soccer?" I felt sad for my son, remembering how cruel children can be when a group of them bands together to make fun of another child.

But Frank spoke up immediately. He started by explaining how the color and shape of a soccer ball helps the players determine its spin. He went on to say that the size of a soccer field is 120 by 100 yards. He knew all about the rules and the form the players take when kicking the ball. The other boy's mouth dropped open as he and the other children got a lesson in soccer. I felt Frank handled this situation quite well. I just praised God that Frank had turned a hurtful conversation into a lesson on the game.

Many times people are eager to share their knowledge with children who are willing to listen. A woman from my Bible study group will come over tomorrow morning to tutor my oldest son in reading, while I have classes with the others. Using a variety of resources can lighten our loads as homeschool teachers. We have the world at our fingertips.

Years ago we had a photography business where we processed and developed 16 mm film. When the NFL went video, our business dwindled down to almost nothing. But during the active years, my husband spent countless hours in the darkroom and lab mixing chemicals in preparation for the evening film development. He always took our children with him and taught them chemistry. We still have that darkroom and photo equipment and perhaps someday we will reopen our chemistry classes as unit studies with other homeschoolers. Resources abound for homeschoolers who look at life as their classroom.

Danielle

Beware of activity burnout! Some parents, in their quest to use as many resources as possible, manage to parcel out their children's entire school day to various classes and end up as unpaid taxi drivers instead of homeschool teachers. The idea behind homeschooling is a total education—life is not divided into various subjects. We are learning patience, time management, new skills, and relationship building all at the same time. Avoid piling a load of activities on your child if those subjects can be incorporated into another study for more complete learning.

Dual enrollment is the latest trend in homeschooling. It is a wonderful opportunity for an exceptional student to earn college credit while studying higher math and science from a professor. Unfortunately, since it *is* college level, it consumes the high school student's time and becomes the primary education instead of a supplement. Sometimes students who are not ready for college become college students just to impress others. I graduated from high school at sixteen with my GED diploma and went straight to college. I could have used another year in homeschool to prepare myself, as the hectic pace of higher education came soon enough. Be careful not to burn out your student and yourself in your eagerness to be involved in as much as you can. Do not allow family and friends to pressure you because they want to see results from your homeschooling. Examine your motives for the activities you select for your children. Relax. Homeschooling should bring joy to your family. There are plenty of resources to help you in the areas where you do not feel confident, but if you have an idea, go for it! Homeschooling opens the door to creativity.   □

3

Schoolrooms and Schedules

Danielle

The curriculum we used our first year turned out to be much too structured for our teaching and learning styles. Some people like the constant accountability of correspondence schools, but it can limit flexibility. This is a fatal mistake for homeschoolers. Often, too much structure kills the fun in learning. Each year, my mother tailored our curriculum to meet our specific needs and interests, especially as we got older. I had a talent for writing, so one year we went through a journalism textbook. My problem area was algebra, so we spent extra time on it, supplementing our curriculum with tapes, games, and anything else that promised to make algebra easier to understand!   □

Donna

I am a very organized person. I write myself notes constantly and always make myself a schedule. If my goals are written out, I feel like I have had a good school day when I see that they were accomplished. The two questions I am most often asked when people hear that I am home-schooled are "What about socialization?" and "What do you do all day?" Both of those questions can be answered by looking at my daily schedule:

6:20	Rise and shine. Okay, maybe just rise.
7:00–8:55	Be at work with Mom, try to greet everyone with a "Good morning."
9:15–9:45	Back from work, breakfast, devotions, bedroom cleanup.
9:45	Grab backpack and walk to schoolroom. (Hey, four bedrooms away can be a long walk.)
12:30	Lunch, cleanup (Mom calls this home economics).
1:45–2:30	Back to work with Mom.
2:45–3:45	Any schoolwork I did not finish (commonly known as homework).
3:45–4:30	Last time we go to work for the day.
4:45–5:45	Do chores, errands, etc. □

People often ask, "How do you get so much done in a day?" I feel that if you are well organized you can accomplish more each day. My job as a crossing guard, which has supplemented the family income for many years, actually helps me to be more organized. After working for different agencies, about four years ago I began working for the county as a guard. After one year with the county, my supervisor put me through a state training program, so I am now a state-certified trainer of crossing guards—a promotion, with higher pay. Instead of being on one corner, I drive past twelve schools throughout central and south Broward

County, checking crossing guards. I do spend a lot of time on the phone, but I enjoy the job. I am up and on the road very early in the morning. While I am driving I take the baby so that my husband, who works the evening shift, can sleep. I also take one older child to help with the baby, in case I run into a situation where I have to fill in for a guard who has not shown up.

This is a special time with the older child and we always have prayer together. We use our hands as our prayer list. The palm of our hand represents praise and thanksgiving. The thumb is closest to us, so it reminds us to pray for those closest to us. The pointer finger reminds us to pray for pastors. The middle finger, because it is the tallest, reminds us to pray for those in authority over us. The ring finger is the weakest, so it reminds us to pray for the weak and unsaved. Finally there is the baby finger which reminds us to pray for ourselves. It is the last one we pray for. Then we have a "praise-around," where we go through the same formula on our fingers, but this time we praise God for something in each category. It is a wonderful way to start the day, and I believe it is the key to our success in organization. If we put the Lord first, he will bless our day. I try to use every minute of the day in a constructive way. Often I am reminded that God gives us only a few short years with our children; we must be good stewards of the time he gives. Just sitting down to converse with your kids can rarely be scheduled, but it is constructive. With the job I have I must be on a schedule. In the morning I am out of the house for at least one and a half hours. Then in the afternoon I am out for one hour. I enjoy getting out of the house and being outdoors. Whether getting your teacher-planner organized, maintaining a clean house, preparing meals, or spending time with your children, organization takes work and self-discipline. A homeschool can function only with careful organization.

Once, while reading aloud with the children, I drifted off to sleep. One of our children had kept me up late the night before. It was an embarrassing moment when Donna gave me a gentle shake and said, "We are all done with that chapter, Mom."

Shaking myself awake I said, "Okay then, let's answer the questions at the end."

Donna replied with a grin, "They have all been answered and turned in to the hand-in box." (The hand-in box is where they put their finished work for me to grade and file.)

The experience was very humbling, yet gave me a good feeling to know that they can accomplish much without constant supervision. It has also been great to see the older ones taking on responsibilities without being told. One thing Donielle, who just graduated from college, says is, "Be sure not to spoon-feed your students. Let them learn to work independently, a skill that they will need in college." She often thanks me for not spoon-feeding her.

Being organized helps you overcome exhaustion. A well-organized schedule actually helps you find time to relax. A neighbor who homeschools often asks one of our daughters to come over to watch her little one while she works on her house or in her studio. So many women today have to work to supplement their family income. On the other hand maybe we can lower our standard of living for the sake of our family. I have talked to many women who have no choice but to work, and my hat goes off to them. We should keep those families in our prayers. Organization is all the more important for them.

I try to remember that my family comes first. I know a homeschool family that is involved in several sports, art classes, 4-H club, and many church activities. I suspect they are headed for burnout. We need to rethink our reasons for homeschooling if outside activities take up all of our time. Many parents feel they must be involved with so much because their children are not in a regular school—that they must do more in order to prove that their children are receiving an adequate education. I am reminded of a story Bill Gothard told about a son who went wayward. The rebellion surfaced after the boy's father had to cancel a fishing trip he had promised. The father justified his absence by saying he was doing the Lord's work. Sometimes we must say no to "good" activities which take us away from home. It is not always a popular response, but sometimes it is the best response. Remember, our families come first.

Before we even began to homeschool, we joined the support group here in Broward County. It is a very well-organized group, with much to offer. I am amazed at how this group has been blessed through the years. The group started with less than seventy families and now has over 520. The group's activities and events will be shared in the coming chapters. I encourage anyone considering homeschooling to join a local support group. As homeschoolers we need to support and encourage each other in the nurturing of our children.

One of the biggest blessings in our homeschool has been doing unit studies with other homeschoolers. All of our unit studies are designed not only to educate the children, but also to build character, friendships, and lasting memories. Every month our children look forward to the various "special days." I plan all of the studies during the summer. Then I simply refer to my planner for each month's topic, gather the supplies, and make copies for everyone. We always have the children bring their own lunches. I know one mom who tried to prepare lunch for all the children, but it was too much for her to do.

Although we have a prepared schedule of activities, unit studies, and group functions for the different age groups in the family, we are always flexible. When something comes up during the year that we feel is important, we try to fit it into the schedule. The summer planning routine includes input from all of our children. They are encouraged to request the subjects they wish to study; they read books, magazines, and encyclopedias to come up with ideas. My sons suggested topics ranging from automobiles to the Confederacy, the military, and spiders. The older girls wanted a unit study on manners. (They said the boys need it!).

Many families co-op and use curriculum such as Konos, Bill Gothard's character-building series, and other similar resources. We try to ensure that all of our unit studies, whether in history, science, language, or the arts, build character traits. We have unit studies for three age groups: three- to six-year-olds, seven- to twelve-year-olds, and thirteen- to eighteen-year-olds; once a month each age group meets here at our house. We do hands-on learning activities about traits such as diligence, patience, attentiveness, love, and generosity. This type of learning sticks with students.

Each unit study is based on the Word of God. The goal for these studies is to build character into each of the children God has loaned us. And what way could be more fun than to bring a group of children into your home and study these qualities together? Many moms who do unit studies or have co-ops trade off week by week. With my schedule I find it easier to do these studies on my own. It is great to watch homeschoolers catch on to the fun of unit teaching. One neighbor down the river began homeschooling two years ago. She is already designing her own investigative unit studies, to which she often invites our two sons and sometimes our daughter. This week they are having a camp-out which will include the study of snakes.

Descriptions of some of the unit studies we have done in the past year follow. You can use these plans with your own children. Remember to use your imagination when planning unit studies. Look around to determine what resources are already available.

Attentiveness Day

On this day we talked about being attentive to the Lord, our parents, and the dangers around us. We read about how Jesus demonstrated attentiveness.

a. We drew a diagram of an ear and talked about listening.

b. We looked into each other's ears with an otoscope (purchased at a drug store).

c. We learned to sing "The Ear Jingle," which teaches the parts of the ear by song. We also did the worksheet that came with it.

d. We learned to spell our names in sign language.

e. We played games like Duck, Duck, Goose; Red Rover; Mother, May I?; and Simon Says.

f. We learned the Ten Commandments from a song.

Obedience Day

On this day we talked about being obedient to the Lord, our parents, and authorities. We talked about how Jesus demonstrated obedience.

a. We sang "This Little Light of Mine," "The B-I-B-L-E," and "In the Light."

b. We talked about being "lights" in the world by being obedient.

c. We made 3-D lighthouse pictures. (Danee designed them out of several layers of construction paper cutouts and aluminum foil for the light.)

d. We made candles. We bought terra-cotta pots and wax in flake form. We used green wax to look like grass. We poured in the wax, inserted the wick, painted leaves on the sides of the pots, and lit the candles.

e. We studied the parts of the eye.

f. We sang a song about self-control from the "Teach Me" tape.

g. We talked about Bible characters who disobeyed and the consequences of their disobedience.

h. The older kids put on a puppet show about obedience.

I. We memorized Ephesians 6:1-3 and earned prizes.

Gratefulness Day

We talked about how that gratefulness is acknowledging that everything we have is a gift from God. Since this unit was near Christmas, we talked about how we are grateful for Jesus. We discussed how God demands gratefulness and how Jesus demonstrated it.

a. We exchanged gifts.

b. We sang Christmas carols.

c. Everyone made two Christmas cards. The first was for the parents and included a list of jobs the children would do for them. The other card was for a sick person. I sent a large envelope of these cards to a shut-in from church and another to a lady who has been ill. We cut up old Christmas cards and decorated them with glitter, glue, construction paper, markers, and crayons.

d. We wrote a song of gratefulness and praise.

e. We wrote the mayor a letter of thanks for all he has done.

f. We made Christmas cookies and decorated them.

g. We made baskets and filled them with citrus fruit and nuts for the children to give to their parents.

Truthfulness Day

We talked about truthfulness and trust. We reviewed the Ten Commandments and discussed the ninth commandment. We talked about how truthfulness is the nature of God, and that lying is the nature of Satan.

a. The older kids had a puppet show they titled "Little White Lies" about a lie that got out of hand.

b. We studied the brain and the heart.

c. We did a newspaper scavenger hunt. I wrote a list of items to be found in the newspaper. Then we spread newspapers out on a long table, and let the children find the items on the list. The first ones finished

received prizes. When we had this hunt for younger children, they had to find pictures in the newspaper, so reading skills were not needed.
d. We sang songs such as "Tame Your Tongue."
e. We played games such as "Two Truths and a Lie."
f. We had a discussion on being truthful to your parents.

Orderliness Day

We discussed the need to be orderly. We talked about how Jesus demonstrated orderliness.
a. With the little children we played with a dollhouse. We discussed how each room in the house has a special function.
b. We made prayer lists.
c. We memorized Bible verses related to orderliness.
d. We painted pictures.
e. We worked with clay. We had contests for the best sculpture, most detailed, most creative, etc.
f. We talked about different types of art.
g. We read about animals who demonstrate orderliness.
h. We talked about proper cleanliness. We encouraged the children to have a daily routine that includes getting dressed, brushing teeth, combing hair, making beds, and doing devotions.

Love and Generosity Day

We talked about the love Jesus demonstrated in dying for our sins. We discussed serving Jesus. This unit study was near Easter, so it fit well.
a. We made Easter baskets.

b. We had an Easter-egg hunt.

c. We made Easter cards and sent them to shut-ins and sick people.

d. We made an acrostic with the name Jesus.

e. We made cross centerpieces to give to the parents. We used old wood, about one inch wide by one-eighth inch thick, and stapled pieces together to make a cross. Then we glued the cross into a pre-painted, round Styrofoam base with a glue gun. We attached silk flowers, lilies, and daffodils to the base with the glue gun. Finally we took a clean white cloth and cut a six-inch-long by one-half-inch-wide strip and draped it over the cross, to show that Christ has risen. It was a lovely centerpiece!

Diligence Day

We talked about how diligence is using all of our energy to accomplish a task. We held a "miniOlympics."

a. We sang songs that got us moving so we could warm up for our games.

b. We played musical chairs on the back porch because it started raining.

c. When it stopped raining, we set up an obstacle course which included hurdles, a tunnel, hula hoops, jump rope, monkey bars, rings, a slide, and mats. The groups were divided by size and age. This was a timed course and we went through it two or three times.

d. We ran a quarter of a mile around the park near our house.

e. We gave out first-, second-, and third-place awards at

lunchtime. We made the awards out of construction paper. We also gave out foil-wrapped chocolate coins.

Indian Unit Study

We have a study on Native Americans. One year a Creek Indian told us the history of the United States from a Native American viewpoint. Another year when we had about twenty-five children meeting for a week of activities, everyone came to our church where each homeschool mom taught for one day. The last few years a Sioux friend has come to our home and taught up to twenty children.

a. Our Sioux friend taught us to make Indian fry bread.

b. She taught the children some words in the Sioux language.

c. She drew pictures of objects which were common to Sioux tribal living, copied them, and let the children color them.

d. The boys made beaded key chains and the girls made necklaces.

e. We made tepee refrigerator magnets.

f. Each child prepared a report on a different tribe and gave it orally.

g. Each child wore a costume, and we had a powwow.

h. We made a real tepee from long wooden poles and drop cloths. We put hay on the floor of the tepee and decorated the tepee with various vegetables. On the walls, we hung life-size posters of Indian life made by the children. They played in the tepee and we kept it up until after Thanksgiving.

i. We sang songs about Indians.
j. Each mom brought a Native American dish which they had researched in their own homeschool. We had a covered-dish luncheon.

This unit study started about nine o'clock and ended about four. It was very educational and fun.

After we list a wide range of ideas, we have a two- to five-day planning session with the older girls. So we could plan somewhat undisturbed, this past summer our oldest son Frank played outdoor games with the younger children. It was not a picture-perfect arrangement; you can imagine the interruptions that happen in a large family. I try to remain calm when such interruptions occur. I feel that with proper instruction and extra patience, children can be taught to help out in all areas. In my "one-room-schoolhouse technique," the older children teach the younger ones. I believe that children should be given responsibility, even at a very young age. Proper training and delegation of responsibility can make family life harmonious.

Granddad built the kids a puppet theater, and now we use puppets in our unit studies quite a bit. Puppets are a good way for shy children of any age to express themselves. Last year the older girls were assigned to make puppets with the children who attended the younger unit-study group. They were also assigned to make up a puppet show about telling the truth. Their personalities and creativity shone. During a love and generosity unit study at Christmastime, the girls dressed up their fingers to look like the three wise men. It was such a cute story that I asked them to do it again at a Christmas party. One daughter had a puppet show about a boy who unwillingly learned a lesson. The next daughter had a show about a very confused puppet that needed direction. This year I assigned the boys to have puppet shows for the youngest age group. There is always plenty of laughter when I allow them to create their own plots.

Dad

With eight children, we have always felt the need for a classroom. This room is a special place that holds many memories. We began our schooling in a converted front porch with unmatched sets of bookshelves. For bulletin boards we used old ceiling tiles turned backwards and mounted to the wall. We had turn-of-the-century desks which we picked up at an auction while on vacation in Kentucky. They each have a hole in the top for an inkwell. The carvings children made in the wood in bygone eras are a history lesson in themselves!

Fun Schoolroom Projects

Even though we are schooling at home, it was never my intention to deprive our children of any needed equipment. Both public and parochial schools can be sources of good ideas. We try to take these and implement them in our own schoolroom. For example, at this time we have no need for an overhead projector in our small classroom—but if we ever do, we will certainly obtain one!

As our family grew, we realized that our classroom could be similar to a regular family room, so we decided to plan it out and spend a little money to make it better than the first one had been. Taking some good ideas from other schools, we decided to install a chalkboard, a chalkless porcelain board, a bulletin board, shelves, and an entertainment center (for the many educational videos and programs). I suspect that in the next few years there will be more programs on satellite geared toward homeschoolers.

Making a Chalkboard

STEP ONE

We purchased a four-by-eight sheet of Masonite. With a circular saw we cut it down to fit on a short section wall in the classroom. Not wanting to waste any of it, we made a small board for the preschool area with the remaining piece.

STEP TWO

We painted the Masonite with several coats of chalkboard paint (purchased at a paint store).

STEP THREE

We mounted the board to the wall with construction adhesive and a few small nails to hold it in place until the adhesive dried.

STEP FOUR

To keep costs down we went to a boat yard and found some scrap lumber that had been used for crating marine engines. One of the best things about this lumber is that it is mahogany, probably from Taiwan or the Philippines. We used this beautiful wood, expensive in this country but common in others, as molding around the chalkboard. We drilled holes and screwed it to the wall. We made the bottom piece larger and drilled holes into it for chalk, and made a notch for the eraser.

Making a White Board

After seeing many of the new schools using chalkless boards or white boards, we decided to make one of those also. We used the same procedure as above for mounting and framing, except we used a white-surface Masonite, such as that used for bathroom walls. We purchased all of these items at a hardware store.

Making the Bulletin Boards

Our first tackboard was a two-by-four-foot ceiling tile, turned backwards and mounted to the wall. It was adequate for our small classroom. For our new larger classroom, we were fortunate to find a four-by-eight piece of paneling being thrown away, and it made a very large tackboard. We used the same procedure to mount and frame it with mahogany. This made all of the boards match and look uniform. We sanded the mahogany frames and gave them a clear finish to add a warm look to our schoolroom.

Making a Building Block Table

One interesting thing we made was our table for Lego-type blocks. After seeing them at a library fair, we really liked the idea but could not afford the table. With this in mind, we found a nice, child-size table being thrown away. We found a one-foot-square Lego base at a toy store, and using contact cement, we attached the base to the tabletop. This makes a great educational place and keeps all of the building blocks in one area!   □

Our new schoolroom was built about five years ago. It has a beautiful skylight that opens and closes with the press of a button. Each child has his or her own workspace. Behind my chair I have bookshelves which hold my books and supplies for the year. I also have a recliner in the classroom; it is a great place to nurse my youngest and to read books to the children. I am amazed at how all of our needs have been supplied. We hardly had to buy a thing. From pull-down maps of the world to a large variety of paper, God has supplied our needs according to his riches. We have divided our schoolroom in half with a divider I made one summer. The smaller section contains the preschool kitchen, with table, chairs, refrigerator, and stove that the little girls can play with and all of the library shelves. Our library continues to grow every year. Danee cataloged all of the books during our planning period one summer when she was feeling especially ambitious. This area also has the Lego table my husband built. Adjoining this is the computer center, with a computer that someone gave us. This hand-me-down went on the blink last month. The Lord supplied us another through NASA's computers for education program. It took some work, but it is now adequate for our needs.

The preschool area gives the younger children a place to play while the older ones study. The little girls can do puzzles, play with dolls, or use activity books—anything but color or paint.

One special memory the children will always hold dear is the family gathered around our ten-foot-long table (custom-built by Dad) eating our noon meal together. Frank works the evening shift and is able to spend the first part of the day at home. After we finish the meal, we read a classic book aloud. Each person reads one page. The nonreaders just listen quietly.

This table stands on our back porch which faces New River. Many days as I look out on the river and see the tides flow in and out and watch the sailboats and power boats come and go, I think of the transient quality of many people's lives these days. Homeschooling provides a closeness I will forever hold dear.

Meals during the school day can be a challenge. At a public school children are fed by trained personnel in a cafeteria. Mom cannot be in two places at once! Some homeschool moms use the once-a-month cooking program. Personally I have not tried this, but we do order our meat from a midwestern food company that ships to us every six months. It costs a little more, but the convenience of having it delivered is wonderful. This is grain-fed beef and poultry, with no steroids or chemicals. Many times I do cook more than one meal at a time, or I cook several meals in the evening. People should find a routine that suits their family. I was recently at one of our homeschool support group meetings where the topic was "A day in the life of . . ." The speakers were four mothers with families of various sizes and different ideas of how to teach their children. Two of the moms spoke about their meal routines. They talked about throwing just about anything on the table to feed their families, saying, "Dig in!" I am very conscious of eating what is good for you. Children are growing and depend on us to teach them proper nutrition and eating habits to carry with them the rest of their lives. I make an effort to have balanced meals and proper food at mealtimes. Prepared food has its place, but it is not what is best for our diet. We eat well-balanced meals with plenty of grains, fruits, and vegetables. We have many classes in our homeschool on preparing and planning wholesome meals, and all take part. Even the two-year-old has to help in the kitchen at cleanup time. She enjoys being part of family jobs.

Our home was built around 1917. It has much character and holds many memories. My husband was thirteen when his parents bought the house. His dad bought it because he and my husband were building a twenty-eight-foot sailing sloop. It took them four years to build and was a valuable learning experience for my husband. We bought the house seventeen years ago with a desire to renovate it. Renovations began six years later and have been going on ever since. As part of their education our children have been helpers in building a two-story garage, stripping hardwood floors in the main house, and even knocking out walls. Frank has taught the girls to cut and hang drywall and how to finish it. The boys have reached an age where life learning has become part of their everyday classroom lessons. He teaches them how to take apart motors, rewire, and even rebuild engines. (I am amazed at my husband's vast knowledge. He is also one of the most patient and wise men I have ever known.) It is wonderful to see the children gather around while he describes the fundamentals of an outboard engine in his big garage/workshop. I am also amazed at how, when renovations began eleven years ago, his ultimate plan was to build our home around the education of our children. Our second oldest, Donna, recently bought a used car at a great price. She thought about rebuilding the engine with her dad, but I think she was afraid that it might make her too dirty or mess up her manicure. By paying a mechanic to rebuild the engine, she has learned that her car is a big money trap. To say the least, her senior year has been educational in the automotive area. She is now thinking about buying a truck!

When we began renovations there was an open breezeway between the garage and the house. We enclosed it, put in a shower, and finished it all with white lattice. With the Lord's provision we purchased a large soft-tub spa so that we can put on our swimsuits and gather as an entire family. It is a wonderful place for all of us to gather. Some of the best times we have had as a family have been in that hot tub. At the close of the day it is a great place to relax, year round, which is an important element of organization. The other day we were visiting friends and their child was fussing about taking a bath. We laughed at how our children race to take a bath. After a shower they cannot wait to get into the hot tub. I love this room, and during the last of several pregnancies I have found much relief here.

Danielle

I was sitting in the living room with a friend the other day, when Dad walked through and said, "When you get a chance will you caulk around the closet we're working on?" My friend laughed at the thought of my doing handiwork, knowing what an uncoordinated person I am. My dad defended me by saying, "In a family this size everyone finds a niche, and Donielle's is caulking." During our many construction projects through the years, we have all been required to lend a hand. I have at various times both enjoyed and resented this. Eventually you discover some job that you do better than anyone else and specialize in it. My hidden talent is caulking. Don't laugh. I am proud of my work. My sister Donna discovered her "construction talent" is taking care of the house and the kids while the rest of us work! Or so she pretends. But that is okay, because Danee and I are not very domestic. There is satisfaction in coming out of your comfort zone and accomplishing something, no matter how small, in an area in which you do not usually shine. The broader our experiences are, the more we grow as students and as people. Homeschooling is all about family. It is learning to do more than just live together or even play together. It is about working together to learn as much as you possibly can in one lifetime. With ten people living in our house, each having some special knowledge they are willing to share, we cannot help but be well-rounded! Dad teaches us to change the oil in our cars and to drive a nail, Mom helps us learn to express our creativity, Donna teaches dance steps, Danee shares sewing and craft ideas, Frank organizes the tools, Daniel tells us everything we have ever wanted to know about Spiderman, Grammy teaches us to be proper hosts and hostesses, and I share concert etiquette. I cannot imagine what my three youngest sisters will have to offer. It is a natural part of family life, but homeschooling makes the most of this family-sharing way of education.

Mom's Typical Schedule
(If not followed, disasters happen.)

6:15	Get up and get going.
6:35	Out the door and on the road.
8:30–9:00	Back at home. Make sure that all have eaten and done their jobs.
9:30	Everyone in the classroom for catechism, hymns, trivia, and our study in the heroes of the faith.
11:00	We break into individual classes. Older children work independently on assignments. Give lessons to the little ones and answer questions for the older ones.
12:00	Lunch. We eat our large meal at noon, almost always planned or prepared ahead. We also share our school accomplishments or problems with Dad.
1:00	Dad reads the Bible aloud. All respectfully listen.
1:20–1:30	We read books aloud, or listen to audiotapes. Children do the dishes.
1:35	Dad leaves for work.
1:45	Mom and Donna leave for work; others read and study.
2:45	Mom returns and works with any child that needs extra help. Grade finished work. Some days, GED study group.
6:30	Light dinner.
7:00	Free time (church classes, etc.)
9:30	Meet on Mom and Dad's bed for Bible memorization and prayer.

(This schedule is not the same on unit-study days or weekends).   □

The first thing in the morning we do our prayers and memorize the Westminster Shorter Catechism. Those important questions young people ask as they grow up can be answered by the catechism, questions such as "Who is God?" and "Why did he create us?" Another thing we study in the morning is sacred hymns. Songs seem to stick with children. One day when the three little girls were jumping on the trampoline, I heard them singing all of the hymns they had learned so far. The trampoline is in the yard facing the river in a place where sound carries. What a testimony, little girls singing about how the law of the Lord is perfect, converting the soul. Maybe someone who needed to hear the words of that hymn heard them.

After we each read one page in our classic book at the close of the noon meal, Frank opens the Bible and reads one chapter. He announced to the children that before they get married they must hear the Bible in its entirety. He has been through it once, so we are in the second reading. In this lies the success of our homeschool. I am convinced that my husband's taking seriously the spiritual headship of this family—his reading, believing, and applying the Word of God to his life—is the reason above all else we have success as a family and success in the lives of our children. The balance is perfect. I believe that if he were not the spiritual leader and did not take the time to read the Bible to us, we would not succeed. After twenty-four years of being married to this man, having eight children, and watching the stages of our lives pass by, I know that his submission in turning the hearts of his children to God is the reason that we see the fingerprints of God on our homeschool. When we began homeschooling, he began reading the Word of God aloud. Ever since that day God has shown great blessing to this family. I am so grateful for this man who has encouraged and lifted me up.

Before going to bed our children memorize Scripture. We use a program that we bought at a homeschool convention two years ago. This is an important routine. I want our final thoughts for the day to be on the Word of God.

We have a reward system which includes Scripture memorization. For every verse that the children learn and recite correctly they receive a point. They can also receive points for a job well done. On Fridays we sing the sacred hymns we have learned and use hand or body movements to express the meanings of the lyrics. At first the boys were too timid to do this, but now they compete for points right along with the girls. They each vote on one another's performance. They score from one to five points on how well each one tried. Acting out the words of the hymns encourages them to express themselves. They must think about the words in order to act them out. Acting out the songs also helps them to memorize the lyrics. The chart on which we mark their points fills up quickly. To redeem the points which they have earned, I have a treasure chest. On Fridays the store is open and they can exchange priced items in the treasure chest for their points. For the older girls there may be nail polish or hair supplies. (I can find many toys and gifts for the treasure chest for very little expense in clearance areas at stores, or after holiday sales.) If an item does not "sell" after a month or so in the treasure chest, I put it on sale for fewer points. This can teach children marketing. Children have to know how to count and spend their points, or they soon learn.

With eight kids the noise level can get very high. When it does, we have what we call "silent restriction." Last week my husband was able to come home for dinner because he was working nearby. All three little girls greeted him at the door telling him of an important event which happened that day. Then nine-year-old Daniel tried to explain the detailed operation of some experiment he was conducting. Ten-year-old Frank also wanted to speak to Dad. And I, too, had some very important information about a phone call which needed his answer in just a few minutes. Unable to listen and reply to everyone at once, he put the children on silent restriction. Then he called on them one at a time to make their speeches. The children realize the importance of a call for silent restriction and respect it. If they break the silent restriction, extra time is added to their restriction. If they speak even once, the silent restriction has been broken. We are fair and realize that little children cannot be restricted for very long, just long enough to calm them down and help them realize that they are being too loud. Car rides can get out of hand and be dangerous if there is too much noise for the driver. A few minutes of silence help the children realize the seriousness of the situation. Last Sunday Frank called a silent restriction during a noisy ride home from church, and after a calm had been reached, he removed each child, oldest to youngest. There was lots of laughter afterwards. Sometimes even friends who are traveling with us or are over playing for the day are put on silent restriction. No one is too old for this call. Even Donielle respects it with a smile. Once I forgot that I had put Ameleigh on silent restriction. She respectfully pointed to her lips to remind me she needed to be taken off restriction. As I did I had to apologize for my forgetfulness.

Respect is an important lesson in our homeschool. If it gets too rowdy, there can be movement restriction also. The children know that they have really gone too far when they are put on one of these, especially the little ones. We rarely need it, but I consider these calls safeguards for sanity in a large family. Sometimes such methods must be used to keep order and peace of mind with all of us. Respect is given and these calls are not permitted to be abused. When young children are bouncing off walls this method is very effective. We teach them to respect us as parents and to respect the chain of authority. They must respect one another, especially if an older child has been put in charge. We trust our children, as they grow, to conduct themselves wisely. I remember while dating my husband that my mom never gave me a specific time to come home. She wisely turned the responsibility of that decision back to me, and told me she would trust me to be home at a reasonable hour. She said, "You won't disappoint me or God."

I remember Chuck Swindoll's claim that he had been successful raising his children because he taught them to be accountable to God. I think that is very important. The children may think "so what?" if Mom says no, but it is different when the Lord says no. We have never had teenage rebellion problems with our children, thank God. In our home when they reach the age where they seem to understand what accountability is, then they need even more responsibility. The Bible does not give us specific instructions on teenagers, but it does speak of youth. Perhaps many of our so-called teenage problems are brought on by society itself. I like to remember that when Jesus turned twelve he was respected and treated as an adult. He was trusted with adult responsibility. In the temple they were amazed at his understanding. I think that when a child reaches that undefinable age of accountability, whether eleven or fourteen, he or she should be treated with the respect of an adult. They should also be given adult responsibilities and trusted with them.

Frank

I want to share with you my experiences in homeschool. I am only in fourth grade, but I have some important things to say. I am always learning something new every day, whether working in the classroom or working outside with my dad. I still remember the first day I started to do schoolwork in the classroom. It was a warm day in September and my brother and I were outside playing with trucks in the sandpile behind my father's garage. When we came into the house, my mother asked me if I would like to sit down and do some work, and I said, "Yes!" First I learned the alphabet. That did not take long. I think that is one of the benefits of homeschool. You can sit down with your mom and learn something quickly.

When I go to homeschool support-group meetings where my family speaks, the one question people always ask at question-and-answer time is, "How do you keep records?" I always get to answer because I am the manager of our records. I run a system I helped develop. Since we began homeschooling, my mom has kept a wooden box that we put our finished assignments in. I have always called it the "hand man" box. That made sense to me. I only found out when I wrote this that it is called the "hand me in" box. That it was a disappointment—all my life I have called it what it wasn't. It does not matter—it is the "hand man" box to me. Once a month Mom grades all the work in the box and gives it to me to file. I file it in order of months. I store it in boxes in the attic above the schoolroom. Mom only keeps the stuff worth keeping. Mom even put a handle on the attic door to make it easy for me. So at the end of every month it is time for me to file.

I like to take school time to go on painting jobs with my dad. This a cool way to learn a trade. If I were in public school, I could not do this type of learning. I look forward to years of growing with my family in homeschool.   □

4

Into High School and Letting Go

My husband feels that "dates" with his daughters are a must. In doing so, he has developed special friendships with them. After many talks with us, they have committed themselves to chastity until marriage. So when the girls reach an age where they are able to date, they make an agreement with Dad to have their prospective suitor ask him for permission to date.

Danielle

To be perfectly honest, I first made this agreement with my dad after attending the Institute in Basic Life Principles Seminar, and now my sisters are stuck with it. It became law. They have both loved and hated me for this. It provides a measure of protection and security, but it scares guys away. I tell my sisters that at least it weeds out the wimps. But we all know that even the bravest of young men quake before my father's intimidating appearance and questions. I think he enjoys it. Who could blame him? Once in a while I even jump into the spirit of the game, but when it comes around to my dates, I remind Daddy that this agreement was made so he could establish a relationship with the young man, not entertain himself! □

Frank asks the would-be where they are going and what time they will be home. There seems to be a great respect for a young lady when all plans must first be cleared with her father. The other evening the girls had a party for their dad. They ordered a cake from the supermarket bakery. The woman who decorates the cakes assumed it was his birthday and wrote "Happy Birthday Dad" on the cake. The girls asked her to correct the mistake and change it to "We love you, Daddy." The lady could not believe the girls would honor their dad for no particular reason. I have mentioned the lack of respect for parents these days, but homeschooling seems to develop respect in these crucial areas. Frank knows that if he does not develop a special relationship with each of his girls, they will look for it in the arms of another man. Dads are wonderful role models, especially those who teach their children the ways of the Lord.

Recently a young man asked Donielle if he could begin dating her. They have been friends for several years. They met at an InterVarsity Christian Fellowship Bible study in the college she first attended. He is a strong Christian. Gary asked Donielle if she thought her dad would give him a hard time when he asked for permission to start dating her. "After all," Gary said, "he does know me." (Donielle should consider getting her master's degree in stage performance. She is quite suited for acting.) She played up her role by telling him what was true (but not necessarily needed information). She told the story of the last young man who asked her out. When he came out from talking to my husband he was shaking and perspiring. Even after that story Gary asked my husband's permission.

My own father happened to be visiting us that evening. We were sitting on the sofa in the living room as my husband and Gary passed by on their way to the schoolroom. I will always remember my dad's twinkling blue eyes and that sly grin when he asked, "Is that the boy? Is he going in there to ask if he may court her?" I knew Donielle would receive some teasing, but I was secure in knowing that Frank was watching over our lives.

I am amazed at how these stages of life go by. At that moment, while looking into my dad's blue eyes, I remembered the day my young, thin, handsome boyfriend, scared and shaking, went into the family room to ask my daddy for my hand in marriage. My oldest brother often recalls the days, many years ago, when I would cry to my mother, "He'll never come back—Daddy told him to get a haircut," or, "It was only nine o'clock when Daddy told him it was time to go home."

You can imagine a brawny, rugged man from the mountains of West Virginia as he told your boyfriend, "It's time to go home, boy."

To say the least, respect for me was given. Mom would say, "He'll be back—if he loves you he'll be back."

Donielle, who was blessed to have graduated from our

homeschool in 1991, graduated from college and is now in graduate school. We are very proud and thankful for the work the Lord has done in her. We look forward to seeing where God will lead her; he has provided for her all the way so far.

Donna graduated from our homeschool this past spring and will enter college in the fall. With her, too, we are proud of the work the Lord has done.

Danee, our third, is in tenth grade. She is very gifted and studious. We cannot imagine how it will be like in the years to come, but with her many talents, it is easy to expect the best.

Graduation and other school-related special events need not be missed simply because a student is home-schooled. Many young people wish to attend regular school because they don't want to miss the exciting occasions, but you can provide for them by planning other similar activities. Several years ago, Donna headed a committee of five other students and planned a most wonderful occasion for older high schoolers. Our group of homeschoolers here in Ft. Lauderdale is full of parents who want to provide alternative field trips and fun-filled teen events for their children. What better way to encourage our young people than to become involved in coordinating memorable occasions. It also allows us to set the tone for occasions in which we might otherwise have no input.

As I think back to our first graduation, Donielle's, I am amazed how the years have passed by. She wore a cap and gown. Actually the gown was her choir robe, and we ordered the cap and tassel with her graduation year on it.

She already had her a class ring, as these are awarded during the junior year. It has her birthstone, with a cross in the middle and "Home School High School—1991" embossed around the stone. After the graduation ceremony we had almost two hundred guests for a buffet dinner. My mother, sister-in-law, and daughters all helped in the preparation. We decorated the church and Dr. Bob Barnes of Sheridan House Ministries was the keynote speaker. He gave a very moving message. Donielle sang for us and delivered her own speech. My brother had a group of teens from his church choir sing. I think Donielle appreciated this event in her life much more than many of the parents did their own graduations.

Her dream is to study music, so she began classes at the local community college. The Lord blessed her with many Christian teachers and professors. She became president of InterVarsity Christian Fellowship. She adjusted well to college life after homeschooling, interacting well with peers as well as adults.

The GED is a wonderful way for homeschoolers to obtain their high school diploma. For three years now, we have held GED study groups in our home each week. They enjoy studying together and it challenges each student. They take a scored test home to their parents to review what they answered incorrectly. This pinpoints their weaknesses and strengths and shows where they need to study more. We review pertinent videos and cover a lot of material in these studies. I do not charge a fee for these classes because it is a challenge and blessing to have others study with my older daughters, so I was surprised at Christmas when one student's grandmother gave me a generous gift with a wonderful note of appreciation for the work I had done with her granddaughter. I was certainly appreciative.

About the GED Diploma

Dr. Patricia Kerensky has been a counselor in Broward County, Florida, for twenty-eight years and has worked in vocational, adult, and community education since 1989. She has this to say about the GED:

There has been public debate about the effectiveness of the General Equivalency Development (GED) high school diploma, so let me point out the overwhelming positives. A viable alternative for graduation for many home schoolers is the GED High School Equivalency Test. This test was developed over 50 years ago to accommodate military personnel who had not completed their high school education. By 1950, civilians realized that this program would be a benefit to everyone who needed a high school equivalency diploma. Today over 3,500 testing centers throughout the United States, Canada, and the U.S. territories administer the GED.

The GED comprises five disciplines and takes seven and a half hours to complete. The GED measures important knowledge and skills expected of high school graduates in the following areas: writing skills, science, social studies, literature and math. Consisting of multiple choice questions and an essay, the test determines one's ability to understand and use information and ideas. Graphs, charts, and reading comprehension compose the format. Though score requirements vary from one jurisdiction to another, most requirements are in terms of a minimum score for each test.

The GED is normed by comparing the knowledge of seniors who graduate from traditional high schools. Thirty percent of these seniors cannot pass the GED test. The U.S. Department of Education states that GED graduates are virtually identical in ability to traditional high school graduates.

I have been involved with the GED testing program for eight years. During that time I have seen over 25,000 adults, ages 16 to 85, receive diplomas in Broward County. Those tested have included students from home schools, gifted classes, and international baccalaureate and advanced-placement programs; housewives; teen parents; immigrants from 98 different countries; and a variety of other adults from all socioeconomic levels.

Last spring, Donna was our second homeschool graduate. She, too, graduated with the GED diploma. We planned a senior party for all the graduating seniors of our support group. We invited new friends and church family, as well as old friends and relatives to celebrate this exciting event in her life. Once again, we were able to use the church to facilitate the event. We had a buffet dinner, a musician to entertain us, and a speaker to encourage the graduates.

As time goes by and things change, so do our lives. This time the graduation ceremony was held at the Florida Parent Educators Association's annual convention in June. This is a wonderful event filled with speakers to support and encourage homeschoolers, along with a large exhibit hall with many curriculum vendors. The graduates all wore caps and gowns on the evening of June 13, when we held our first statewide graduation ceremony. How far things have come since our first daughter graduated! There was a keynote speaker, and my nephew gave a speech as the recipient of the Craig Dickenson Memorial Scholarship, named in memory of our late homeschool lobbyist.

Donna's Senior-Year Schedule

March	The parents of the seniors in the Broward County Parent Support Group have the first planning meeting for the senior celebration.
April	We order and pick up our caps and gowns. We have senior pictures taken.
May	The seniors' parents have a second meeting where we make final plans and delegate responsibilities. We purchase decorations and contact the musician to sing for the evening's entertainment. We plan the menu.
June 7	The senior celebration is held at our church from 6 to 10 P.M.
June 13	The senior graduation is held in Orlando.

We ordered our graduation invitations from a print shop when Donielle graduated, but for Donna's graduation and senior celebration, we designed our own on the computer.

What about socialization? Everywhere I go that seems to be the first question people ask when they find out we are a homeschooled family. Many will take my teenagers aside and ask them, "Really now, do you like homeschool?

Do you miss your friends? What about that high school experience? Do you think that you will be able to get along with others in college, or will you be a wallflower? Won't you miss those wonderful occasions like prom?"

I remember my own high school experience. It was not all that nice. The prom was an expensive event, a very worldly function. We felt that as Christians (Frank was then my boyfriend), we were compromising by attending. This was in the 1970s, and drugs and free love seemed to be the norm with teens from public school. I am glad the Lord had his hand on us even then. That kind of prom is not what I want for my Christian teenagers. It is hard enough to maintain one's walk with the Lord in this world which desires our children to accept its low standards.

Since people ask my teenagers what they really think of homeschooling, I'll let them speak for themselves.

Donna

When people ask about homeschooling, the first question is almost always, "What about socialization?" Well guess what? Homeschooled kids are just like everyone else.

Sixth grade was a hard year for me. It was the year I got braces. It was the year my body decided to mature. It was at the beginning of that year that I hated homeschool. I felt that I had no friends. I felt like there wasn't anything I could do that one of my sisters could not already do better. I thought my problems would go away if I could go to traditional school.

Then one day Mom came back from a support-group

meeting excited about a new prospect for me. There was going to be a newspaper for homeschooled kids, written by the teens and preteens in our support group. We called our newspaper "Kids-2-Kids." We met every month, and Mrs. Vicky, the mother who organized this paper, presented a list of topics she wanted us to cover. She let us choose which topic we would like to write about, on the assumption that if the writer was excited about the article it would be well done. She gave us a star for every article written and presented us with a trophy at the end of the year, based on our effort. We also put on a drama production in which we each played a different historical character. We had to research our character, write a script, and memorize it. We charged twenty-five cents admission and gave the money to Florida's homeschool lobbyist. As I look back on that year, I am so glad that my parents made the extra effort so I can say I love homeschooling!

When I was thirteen I wanted to be a cheerleader. I tried to join a city league, but I was too old; so they asked me if I would like to coach. I coached girls ages six through eleven. There was an incident where a coach from one of the opposing teams asked her girls to do cheers that put our team down. I asked my girls not to do cheers that put down other teams, and not to pay attention to other cheerleaders when they were doing that cheer. By doing this I gained respect. My team won the cheerleading championship both years that I coached.

For three years now, homeschoolers in Broward County have had their own yearbook. We start putting together the yearbook in October. My dad holds a photo workshop for anyone interested in learning about photography. He teaches the mechanics of the camera, proper lighting, and an overall approach to taking good pictures. Then we get some real hands-on experience. Each person signs up for taking one day of yearbook pictures, and they work right alongside my dad who is taking the professional photos. Later, when the material is assembled, we get to help with the layout.

Each month someone from the parent support group plans a teen social activity. The most popular is the mall scavenger hunt. We usually get along pretty well. We make an effort to meet and greet new homeschool teens. I think the most frequent questions homeschooled high schoolers ask each other are, "Are you going to homeschool all the way through high school?" If they are, the next question is, "How are you planning to graduate?" and, of course, "Where are you going to college?"

Each year in the fall, students throughout the country gather at their school flagpole at 7 A.M. I organized a small group to gather at the flagpole in front of our city hall. We held hands and earnestly prayed for our country, the school year, our support group leaders and our teachers. Then we sang a few praise songs. What an experience we were able to have because we are homeschooled.

I have always been active in church. There was always something exciting about attending vacation Bible school, memorizing Scripture verses, earning points for our team, and singing the Bible school songs. So when I was too old to attend, I became a teacher. I also taught Pioneer Clubs and a Wednesday night catechism class. It is very rewarding when a child looks up and smiles, showing deep appreciation for all of your time and effort, or when they surround you with hugs, all trying to be the first to show you their work. I once chaperoned a camping trip for middle schoolers. What an experience! I was in a tent with five giggling girls. We endured the boys throwing frogs in our tent and anything else that would make the girls scream. When I finally fell asleep, I was awakened by the girls' chatter. I understood their desire to talk but also knew the rest of the camp needed some sleep. I told the girls that they could only talk in whispers. After that weekend I believe it will take a couple of years to recover my desire to camp! I attend my church youth group and my cousin's church youth group. Involvement in church activities is a good source of positive socialization.

Through our homeschool, I have had the opportunity to help cheer the elderly at nursing homes. At Christmas we visit and sing carols, do dances, recite poems, or teach them a new song. They are our best audience. Some of them are so starved for attention—their families do not come to see them very often. At one particular nursing home, a sweet lady always begs us to come back. I remember when we went caroling around December 15th and a lady who was convinced it was Christmas Day kept asking us what Santa had brought. One afternoon I was able to serve tea. As I served they asked me if I was Irish because of my red hair. I attempted to explain that I am mostly Scottish and English, but several ladies had already broken into a chorus of "When Irish Eyes are Smiling," and I could not ruin their fun. I was told by a lady who clung to my arm that they do not often get visitors. She had dressed up for the occasion in a big hat with pink flowers. I always look forward to these visits; I go to touch their lives, but somehow they always end up touching mine.

I hate math. It is definitely my worst subject, so every Monday I tutor a girl in math. Being a math tutor keeps me on my toes because I have to make sure I understand every concept before I teach it. Each Monday we begin our class with prayer, asking God to help us understand and remember everything we learn. I help the students review with multiplication flash cards. I use a point system: every correct answer earns a point. Prizes are awarded when a certain number of points is earned. Then we work on division and fractions to the tempo of music. Tutoring has sharpened my math skills and encouraged me in the subject I like the least. □

Dance

This year, among other things, I organized a thirty-hour famine. It is a hunger-awareness fast. We asked people to sponsor us and then fasted for thirty hours. The proceeds went to World Vision, who organizes this national event and uses the money to feed the poor. We slept at our church that night and had a mall scavenger hunt on Friday night. Then Saturday morning we held a car wash to earn more money for World Vision. At every mealtime we had a Bible study instead of food. After that we put together baskets and dropped them off in front of houses in poor neighborhoods. With donated food we went down to Tent City, a large tent downtown where homeless people can stay. We fed the homeless people out of the back of a van. It was very rewarding. □

Danielle

When people used to ask me where I went to school I said Riverview Academy if I was not in the mood to answer questions. If I answered that I was homeschooled, I was sure to be asked more questions. "What is homeschooling?" was a pretty common question back then. Then there was the socialization question. People seem to have a difficult time realizing that school is for learning, not playing with your friends. I always went through the list of activities I was involved in and mentioned that I had enough siblings to take care of socialization.

One trait that often sets homeschoolers apart is their ability to talk to adults. This is a natural outcome for students who receive one-on-one attention, versus the average school situation, where a student receives personal attention only if they are having a problem. Communicating with adults is difficult if you function only in a teen subculture. Homeschooling provides the opportunity to develop the conversational skills needed for college and adult life.

This kind of maturity, which I see developing in my sisters also, provided me with opportunities for leadership at a young age. I was asked to teach a Pioneer Club group of first and second graders when I was fourteen. I thought I was too young, but the directors kept encouraging me to try it, so I did. I loved it! I taught for three years after that. Writing my own lesson plans, learning to discipline kids, and having the awesome experience of leading a child to the Lord all contributed to preparing me for adulthood and future jobs I would hold. I have worked for several summers at a day camp. Last year I was promoted to arts and crafts director. They had noticed my knack for seeing what materials we had lying around, and creating something out of them. This "skill" was developed from teaching Pioneer Clubs and vacation Bible school during my middle and high school years at a church with limited resources and a small budget. □

We feel Donna has been prepared in the essential areas because she has been homeschooled through high school. She has a keen sense of direction for her life, she is responsible with her finances, and she can communicate with people of all ages. She has strong character and a godly set of values. She believes Jesus Christ is Lord in all areas of her life. The arrow has been cocked and is ready to launch. The key factor to success in her raising is her schooling at home. This past summer she had her first test on how she would do on her own. She went on tour with the Continentals from early June to late August. God does prepare parents for letting go and allowing those birds to fly, but this was a summer I will never forget.

The Continentals came to our church in the spring of 1996. I had no idea that after the concert our two oldest daughters were inside auditioning.

Donna

When the Continentals visited our church in March, Donielle and I thought it would be interesting to get some information. After filling out the application, the assistant director asked me to come to the piano for a quick audition, explaining that there would be no obligation. I decided to give it a try. Afterward he explained the costs and paperwork I would need in order to travel with the group. I kept telling myself that this would never work. I could never raise that much money, and even if I could, I did not think that my parents would let me leave for that long. But in the back of my mind was a reassuring thought that if it was the Lord's will, it would all work out.

I was at work when someone from the Continentals called the house. They told my sister that I had been accepted, and they did not need me to send in an audition tape. (The man who had auditioned me waived the need for that.) After my parents gave their consent, I sent in my application, along with a musical and a pastoral recommendation. I also wrote to the missions committee of our church and to some individuals, explaining about the trip and how much it would cost. In order to go, I needed to raise $3,500 plus plane fare and spending money. One particular elder in our church had great faith that I would be doing good if I went on the trip, and he directed me to a few benefactors. When the Continentals next called, they said that my application, recommendation, and other papers had been processed, but they still needed a $350 deposit. It was due the next day! My mom and I sat down and prayed. We asked the Lord to provide the money by the next day if it was his will that I go. We cried together and shared our fears about the summer, if I did end up going on the tour.

At 4:45 the next afternoon my Sunday school teacher called and asked how much I needed to get started! I explained the deposit situation to him, and he said he would provide the money. He has a very big heart for youth. By the time I got off of the phone and ran outside to tell Mom, it was five o'clock. As I told her about the call, she grew excited and asked me what time it was. Confused, I told her it was five o'clock. She then told me that she had prayed that if the money came by five, she would be able to let me go, knowing it was God's will.

Lots of trials and tests of faith led up to the departure day. My entire family and all of my grandparents accompanied me to the airport. I was scared. I had never taken such a big step before. I was flying by myself across the United States to a place I had never been, to meet and spend two and a half months with people I had never met. The only thing that kept me from running back into the plane terminal was the realization that God had given me such a unique opportunity to use my summer for him. As my Mom gave me one last hug she told me there would be a special friend who would comfort me on the plane. She said that she would like to hear all about this person when I called. Donielle hollered to be sure and eat right, then there was a chorus of "We love you," and they were out of sight.

With tears streaming down my face, I walked down the airplane aisle, looking for my seat. When a lady finally sat next to me I offered a forced smile and turned away. How was I going to get through the summer if I was homesick before the plane even took off? When we were in the air she asked if I was all right. I explained that I was going on a missions trip with the Continental Singers, but I was already lonesome for my family. She told me about her daughter who had gone on a mission trip and what a wonderful experience it had been for her. Before I knew it, we had stopped in Atlanta. I was not scheduled to change planes, but once we landed they announced a mandatory plane change. The lady who had befriended me went well out of her way to make sure I was headed in the right direction. She even came back to make sure I was boarding the right plane.

As I was waiting to board I looked over at a young man. There seemed to be such a peace about him; I wondered if he was a Christian. Then I wondered if he might be touring with the Continentals, but I pushed aside that thought as silly. I smiled at him, then boarded the plane. When we arrived in Los Angeles, I grabbed my pillow and backpack and headed for the baggage claim, where a Continentals official was supposed to meet us. Before I reached the baggage claim I saw a group of people holding signs that said "Continental Singers." They told me to get my bags and come back to where they were waiting. As soon as I returned with my luggage, I was cheerfully greeted by the young man I had wondered about in Atlanta. He admitted that he, too, wondered if I was going to travel with the Continentals.

From then until the early hours of the morning, there was a great deal of activity as we traveled to and got situated in the college campus where we would train for the next week. By the time I got to bed I was exhausted, lonely, and scared. I cried myself to sleep. When I woke up in the morning I thought if I left then I would not regret it, after all I did not even know anyone yet. Not knowing what else to do, I called home. When my dad answered I explained how homesick I was. He gently told me I needed to give it more time, especially since all that money had been spent. I agreed to keep trying, since just talking to them made me feel better. They told me I could call every day if I needed to. I did end up calling all eight days of rehearsal camp.

While at rehearsal camp, we had to learn fifteen songs, nine dances that went with the songs, the order of the program, and our riser positions. We were also assigned the jobs we would have once we were on the road. Along with another girl, I would have to unload and iron all fourteen of the girls' concert outfits.

For three days, from 9:00 A.M. to 9:00 P.M., we learned choreography from an energetic professional dancer. We learned the hardest dance first. I felt frustrated because before I could master one step, he would go on to the next one. We had only those three days to get all of the dances down to perfection. We stopped only for meals! Between dancing all day and walking up and down the hills of the campus, we really got a good workout!

Rehearsal camp taught the endurance that we would need for two and a half months on the road. The showers in the girls' dorm were crazy. Whenever someone was in the shower you could almost guarantee a scream of surprise. Every time someone flushed the toilet, very hot water came out of the shower. Not hot enough to burn you, just enough to make you squeal. A few times we girls from Tour O got together at about 11:30 and had pizza or shared candy.

With a team of twenty-six people, there had to be some rules. We rotated seats so that we sat with a different person everyday. We were not allowed to have a best friend or any boy- or girlfriends while on tour. We were only allowed to give side hugs to people of the opposite gender. If we left something in our dressing rooms, it cost a quarter an item to get it back, unless it was a Bible or garment bag—they cost more. In order to keep the bus clean, a pillow was the only thing we could leave in our seats when we got off. Anything else also cost us.

Being crammed on a bus all day, every day, with twenty-six people, some feelings of hostility and anger were bound to arise. We had to learn to get along despite all of that. Before each concert we were given time to encourage one another or work out any interpersonal problems, so that we could give our all during the concert.

We had the opportunity to visit Mexico on two different afternoons. One of the afternoons we were able to shop—that was a learning experience! As we walked through the streets, people tried anything to lure us into their shops. One man hollered, "Come and buy something, so I can buy tequila!" As I walked through the streets I remembered the unit study we had done on Mexico—I had not imagined I might actually go there. The second afternoon we sang at San Javier Temple, then at an orphanage and the kids, in turn, sang for us. Then we all went out to the playground! Some of our guys started a basketball game, while the rest of us played ball, jumped rope, or climbed on the jungle gym. The children spoke only Spanish, and I knew only a few Spanish words, but that did not matter. We were able to communicate through smiles, hugs, and hand gestures.

We were in Atlanta for a week during the Olympics. We sang mostly inside or outside of a church. One day we went into Centennial Park to sing. The words of the song we were singing said, "I'm looking up, the sun is shining, there's not a cloud in the sky," but as we were performing it started to rain. That got a laugh from the crowd. Several hours later, a few feet from where we had been performing, a bomb exploded. God had protected us.

We also visited Targetworld, a training camp for kids before they go out on mission trips. Most of these kids were from other countries. We thought the conditions were horrible. The food was gross, and to quench our thirst, they gave out little bottles of purple juice, hot and nasty. The bathrooms had only two open, freezing showers. The toilet stalls hardly ever had toilet paper. Yet through all our complaining, the Lord was able to show us how blessed we are. For some of the countries represented, these conditions would have been luxurious. Through our Bible memorization I was reminded of Matthew 6:28-30, "And why do you worry about clothes? See how the lilies of the field grow. They do not labor or spin. Yet I tell you that not even Solomon in all his splendor was dressed like one of these. If that is how God clothes the grass of the field, which is here today and tomorrow is thrown into the fire, will he not much more clothe you, O you of little faith?" How we constantly take for granted that which the Lord has provided.

We learned also another important lesson at Targetworld while a playing game with a group from Korea. The rules were: 1) Women were never to look men in the eye. 2) Animals were valued more than women. 3) We were never to use our left hands. The Korean kids played the missionaries who were trying to share the gospel. But the missionaries realized they could not just come in and push their ways upon us; they had to understand our village first.

My sister Donielle sent a big package of snacks while we were at Targetworld. Everyone was truly grateful to her. Whenever someone received a package, they had to sing a solo for it. Donielle had written on the package, "If she has to sing for this, make her sing 'Blue Moon' in a mouse voice." (That was something I had done that really amused my family.) I sang the chorus once, much to my embarrassment. When I left Targetworld, the girl who had been my partner gave me a Korean doll as a parting gift.

At the end of the summer when I stepped off the plane in Ft. Lauderdale, my family and a group of friends were waiting to greet me. They held signs with my picture that said, "Have you seen this girl?" What a crazy bunch! That was a summer I will never forget: I learned what being a missionary is all about and began to understand the meaning of faith and of totally trusting God. ☐

Donielle

As soon as teenagers enter high school they start needing more money. It is one of life's simple rules. Becoming an adult means increasing expenses, and I was no exception. I wanted to work, but my parents wisely did not want a job to interfere with my schoolwork. I have seen a number of homeschooled high schoolers take advantage of their flexible schedules to get jobs, which then become more important than school.

But we found I could work three days a week, two

hours a morning, caring for an elderly neighbor. The job was not difficult, except perhaps emotionally. I comforted her as she shared her depression over how Parkinson's Disease was stripping away her freedom and mobility. I cried with her over the indignity of my having to wipe her after she went to the bathroom. She shared stories of being a Navy nurse during World War II, of being widowed at a young age, and of her personal spiritual odyssey. From that job I learned patience, compassion, and how to encourage others.

A money-management course had been part of my curriculum in my first year of high school, and now I was able to test my management skills with the money I earned. I faithfully added to my savings account, and that money helped me through college. This was my first experience of having a steady income, since my parents never believed in giving allowances. I was raised with the understanding that my parents do not owe me anything, and this has built in me a healthy respect for my parents. Sound a little harsh? Not if you take a good look at the teen rebellion epidemic in our society. Their attitude says the world has not done enough for them. I would respond to my generation by saying, "Get over yourselves!" Or to quote my friend Margarita, "Get off it, or it's going to hurt when someone pulls you off!" The Bible says, "Naked I came from my mother's womb, and naked I will depart" (Job 1:21).

Through middle and high school I also earned money while working with my father in his side business, sports photography. I assisted him on photo shoots and helped with bookkeeping, but my favorite part, besides customer relations, was filming football games. I spent three seasons going to games with him and training on the 16 mm camera. When I was fifteen, he began assigning me my own games to film. I was finally a real cameraman! I also learned video filming, which has proven useful for earning extra cash through college.

Homeschooling is more than a method of education. If that's all it is, then we should have simply written a how-to book. Instead, we have written a how-we-did-it book. That is because homeschooling is a life philosophy. It is a question of who is responsible for education, of how we learn and why we learn. It is a way to teach your children to think. The goal is to feed them answers that spark more questions, which sparks creativity, which sparks resourcefulness, which sparks answers, which sparks more questions. What good is it to sit in a classroom and hear answers to questions one has not yet asked? So many students are apathetic to education for this very reason. Let's make students curious about something before we give them information that they will perceive as meaningless—then we will not have to work nearly so hard at making learning fun. When you have the desire to know and understand, it is fun to discover the answers!

Education can become nothing more than a trivia game, a competition of who knows the most encyclopedic facts. There is, of course, nothing wrong with rote memorization of things you will likely use later on. Mother had us memorize a great deal that way: multiplication tables, U.S. presidents, the state names and capitals, the books of the Bible. But that was not an end in itself. It was a means of readying ourselves for a bigger debate: higher math,

American history, U.S. geography, Old Testament theology. We were not learning these facts so we could know a lot and show off (although these things do impress cynical relatives); they are merely a starting point to bigger things. That is what homeschooling is supposed to do: prepare you for bigger things! It gives students tools that will last a lifetime.

I would be interested to know if homeschooled students have better problem-solving skills than the average traditionally schooled student. My experience suggests that they do. I am aware of the resourcefulness that it developed in me. In my first year of college I discovered that I needed more money. I was not working because my parents discourage anything that might take precedence over schoolwork. But I needed money, so I surveyed what I had: eight years of dance lessons and a following of admiring little girls. That certainly could translate into money. I used our church fellowship hall for a studio and taught a six-month class with a recital at the end, complete with sparkly leotards and tutus. Resourcefulness is a survival skill! □

5

At Home in a Big Family

Holidays are incorporated into our school days, and we have three birthdays in October. The gifts for the three are neatly arranged in a corner of the living room. If you multiply birthday gifts for three people by eight, you can see that this is a busy month. And imagine what Christmas looks like! I have had people comment that we really start Christmas early. You should see the gifts! A family of ten plus two grandparents who all give gifts to each other equals a lot of presents. Sometimes friends come over on Christmas morning just to watch the children's reactions when they open gifts.

As our family grew in size, I promised myself that I would always let the children know how special they are as individuals. I tell them they are special not only in our eyes, but also in the eyes of the Lord. So this family celebrates! Birthdays and holidays can be celebrated on a bare-bones budget if you are creative. We make many of our gifts and teach the principle of giving rather than receiving. One of the most creative persons in our home is Danee. She has much to say about birthdays and holidays.

Danee

"Look Danee," Mother said as we were walking through the drug store, "all of the Valentine's Day stuff is half price."

I asked why we wanted valentine stuff when Valentine's Day was over, and Mom answered, "We could use the stuff that has hearts for Donna's sixteenth birthday party in March."

We sorted through the clearance items and found stickers for the invitations we were planning. We found candy roses and other silver-wrapped candies. Closer to her birthday, we went to a party store and found (in the clearance, of course) napkins and plates with hearts that said "Sweet Sixteen." We also picked up some plastic wine glasses for old-fashioned root-beer floats.

Birthdays are so important. They are a time not only to receive gifts, but also a time set aside to honor that person, to celebrate that they were born and live on this earth!

"It is so hot out," said Mom, as she stepped into our unair-conditioned car. It was the middle of August, and in Florida the temperature can be almost unbearable. In order to survive in our car without air-conditioning, we sometimes find it necessary to stop for a forty-two-ounce fountain drink, which my youngest sister Darleen will manage to drink down to the last drop if no one stops her.

"So what are we going to do for Ameleigh's sixth birthday party?" I asked.

"Well," Mom said, "we'll have to hold it somewhere that is air-conditioned since our house isn't."

I thought for a little while, then ventured an idea. "What about a water party? We could fill the kiddie pool with bubbles and pull out the Slip-n-Slide."

Mom ran with the idea. We decided to add Play-Doh and finger-painting stations and finish off with a swim in the two little pools we have.

At the party I organized an obstacle course.

"I want to be the first one," yelled one little girl.

"All right," I said, "You must swim around the first pool, walk around the second, crawl across the Slip-n-Slide and come back to me. The person with the fastest time wins."

We gave them prizes of popcorn and peanuts wrapped in plastic wrap, adorned with curly ribbon, with a pencil and tiny notepad tied to it. Everyone had a blast. They were smeared with finger paint and Play-Doh and enjoyed splashing and cooling off in the pools.

I enjoy clearance shopping for party supplies. I not only save a whole lot of money, but it is also fun and rewarding to get a bargain. And it is challenging to find them! Suppose I find something that would make a good decoration or party favor with fish designs on it. My theme is now fish. If I find something with boats on it, I might make it a water theme party. I could give goldfish crackers as party favors, find inexpensive boat stickers, add a little candy, put it all in sandwich bags, and decorate with curly ribbons. I could also make a large personalized banner with boats and fish around the words "Happy Birthday" (or whatever the sentiment is). I like to make my banners by taping large white pieces of paper together and then lettering with markers or construction paper cut-outs. Then I draw pictures or cut them out of magazines.

In our house we have so many birthdays that we always

keep leftover streamers and balloons on hand. I love confetti—it adds a special, fun touch. I put it in invitations, sprinkle it on tables, or throw it.

One night during dinner Donielle said, "I want to have a birthday party for Jennifer, but I don't have a whole lot of money to spend."

The truth was, she did not have any money to spend. Like most college students Donielle hardly ever had any money, despite all her scholarships awarded for talent and excellent grades (by her second year of college she had a 4.0 GPA). Jennifer was turning twenty-four, and she was a good friend of the family. "I have a good idea," Mom said, "Why don't you have a Mexican party? I could make a big Mexican salad."

Mom's Mexican salads are delicious. She puts down a layer of tortilla chips, adds fresh spinach, guacamole, tomatoes, cheese, salsa and a couple of finely chopped jalapeños.

About a week before the party Donielle and I made a piñata that looked like a man wearing a sombrero. We made it from a large balloon covered with cut strips of newspaper and watered-down white glue. We dipped the newspaper strips in the glue one at a time and covered the balloon with three thick layers of the wet paper. Then we cut a piece of cardboard into a circle and cut a hole out of the middle. We placed it on the balloon so that, with part of the balloon sticking through, it looked like a sombrero. Then we added more layers of paper to hold it all together and let it dry overnight. Then Donielle painted a face, hair, mustache, and other features and cut a slit in the back through which to insert the candy. She named our masterpiece Tito.

"All the Mexican plates are so expensive," Donielle whined as we walked through a discount party supply store.

"Why don't we just make the plates and cups ourselves?" I suggested.

"How?" she asked in a dry tone.

I suggested that we take plain white paper plates and cups and draw jalapeños and some other Southwestern pictures around the edges with colored markers. Using the materials we had at home, we made streamers out of adding-machine paper by drawing the same pictures we had drawn on the plates and cups. It was a great party, and Jennifer felt very special.

I love having parties. If I see any reasonable cause, I take it and run. My close friend Bethany had a birthday coming up so I decided to throw her a party. After searching through some magazines I chose a theme of flowers and gardens. I started by gluing white paper petals to the underside of yellow disposable plates. Mom found cups with yellow and white flowers and a little green on them. Now we needed to find napkins to match the blue-green leaves on the cups. I already had pink napkins at home, so we added a package of blue-green ones. Laid on top of one another with alternating colors, they were beautiful. I laid a plastic fork and spoon on top, tied the napkins around with a pink and white bow, and fastened a flower onto the bow.

For party favors I used sticks of gum, flower stickers, seed packets, and little bottles of bubbles wrapped in green tulle. I put all the party favors in strawberry baskets with yellow crinkle stuffing in the bottom. I intertwined flowered ribbon into one row of the basket and made a bow for the side. For an extra favor, which everybody ate before they left, I made a flower cookie. I put a popsicle stick into a piece of soft chocolate candy, wrapped cookie dough around the individual candies, and flattened them out. While the cookies were baking, I cut large marshmallows into four pieces each. The cut-marshmallow edges turned up to look like flower petals. When the cookies cooled I iced them with colored icing, put the marshmallow petals on, and squeezed a dot of yellow icing into the center.

By being homeschooled, we are better able to celebrate birthdays because we have time for kitchen-science classes, and my mother allows us to experiment. We are also closer to each other than we might be if we went to a public or private school, because we spend a greater amount of time together bonding. Having a close family makes everyone want to celebrate each other's birthday.

Every year near Valentine's Day we make decorated valentine holders out of paper plates or envelopes. Then we make and distribute Valentines for each person in the family. During school we have a little party and we look through our holders. Then for lunch we have some special food such as heart-shaped pasta, garlic toast cut into hearts, or sandwiches pressed with a cookie cutter. Whatever it is, it is always special.

Easter is also a special time for me. The girls get new dresses, and the boys get new shirts and ties to wear on Easter Sunday. The night before we color our eggs. In our family it takes about six dozen. To boil that many eggs, we use a giant pot. Easter morning we rush into the living room to see what is in our baskets. After we look at all the candy (and sneak a piece or two), we get ready for church.

(Typically several family members go to church with Easter-egg-colored hands!) When we get home, everyone has to stay in their church clothing for the camcorder during our egg hunt. It sometimes takes a while to find the camera, the battery, and a blank tape, but finally someone yells, "Remember the rules: little kids get a head start, and big kids cannot grab the easily-found eggs. There are seventy-two hard-boiled and fifty plastic eggs. On your mark, get set, GO!"

When we can't find any more, we all come in for an egg count. Sometimes we miss two or three and are sent out to look again.

"I found one!" exclaims Daniel, and the hunt usually ends on that note. The last egg or two will be found in the next couple of months if they are plastic, or they will be eaten by a raccoon or some other wildlife if they are real. The family then gets together at my grandmother's house or somewhere else for dinner, with ham or turkey, Grammy's green beans, pickled eggs and beets, mashed potatoes, and pineapple-apricot delight.

One school project that we all love is putting together a scrapbook for the year or for the summer. Not only do we collect photos, but also pamphlets, ticket stubs, drawings, receipts, napkins—almost any souvenir. At the end of the summer or year we buy a photo album, and I get out my zig-zag scissors and some colorful construction paper and get to work. Since my dad is a photographer, we have learned that we should not cut photos, so I try not to cut them unless they are really bad or unless I have the negative. I trim the construction paper and describe on it what the photo is about. Sometimes I add stickers, and my beautiful scrapbook is done! It is something that we can look back on in the years to come and remember the fun times with the family in our homeschool. It also is a good addition to our school portfolio, which is required by law in Florida.   □

Big families require a lot of organization, and homeschooling intensifies that requirement. I find that each day needs special consideration. For example, Saturday is cleaning day, even for our youngest child. Each person in the family has a responsibility. I put together a cleaning guide so those old enough to read may refer to it. Anyone can write one of these; you just need to go from room to room in your house and decide what needs to be accomplished in that room. Write down this list with instructions on how to do each job. You can even draw simple diagrams. Put it all together in book form and add a colorful cover.

It is good for a child's self-esteem to know what is expected of him and to accomplish these tasks for Mom and Dad. We usually complete our Saturday jobs by midafternoon, allowing time for transition to family time, or a date night for Mom and Dad. With a large family there are always babysitters available, but sometimes the older children have their own social agendas planned. But when we want to go out, they are always considerate of our need to be alone with each other. This is important when you homeschool. Considering that you are with your children so many hours a day, you need plan special times with your spouse.

Organization requires preparing your family for Sunday-morning worship. We lay out the clothes we are going to wear the evening before. We try (and sometimes fail) to get the children to bed on time. We also plan an easy breakfast so we can try to arrive to church on time. This is an area we need to work on! Frank and I feel that children should be taught to worship with their families unless they are being disruptive. I will never forget one Sunday morning when we were walking up the church aisle with our son Frank, who was just a baby. We were so proud of his excellent behavior in church. There was a little girl in the congregation who had been born about the same time as little Frank. She seemed to be fussy baby. As we passed Melanie, she let out a scream. We sat down in the pew and wondered what was wrong with her that day. Then we noticed a handful of Melanie's hair in Frank's hand! We were certainly humbled by Frank's behavior.

Laundry seems to be a universal problem. We usually assign the bulk of the laundry to one person as a Saturday job, but all the children are required to help put the clothes away. To keep the laundry under control we must wash and dry at least one load a day. This can be folded and neatly put into a basket in the laundry room, but on Saturday it must all be put away and the laundry room cleaned and mopped. Socks can be a thorn in the flesh when it comes to household organization—we have an entire basket full of unmatched socks! Last Christmas Danee tried to think of a craft she could make using unmatched socks. Puppets were all she could come up with. Last Saturday we were landscaping and found several long-lost socks in various parts of the yard. I still wonder how they got there.

At a fall festival our two sons and one of our daughters

entered a pie-baking contest with high hopes of winning. They spent a full afternoon preparing fruit pies. They did not win, but they had a great time making the memory. Their pies were very tasty for inexperienced cooks. All of my children enjoy kitchen science, but especially the boys. During the holidays we have days where we cook many different dishes and desserts. I utilize my one-room-school-house technique of teaching as I hand out assignments, encourage the following of directions, and allow for individual creativity. I always emphasize the responsibility of cleaning up, but I try not to worry over spilled flour or sugar. As you teach the older children to be responsible and help the little ones, fewer accidents happen. Many times we have a kitchen-science class where we plan and prepare the noon meal for the next day. It might include a stew, a loaf of homemade bread, and a homemade dessert. Sometimes we use a Crock-Pot and put a meal in before bedtime. This makes things easy at noon when we stop for lunch, our main meal of the day.

Danielle

Multilevel teaching is not easy, but it comes more naturally than you might expect. In a large family this is the only way homeschooling can work. Teaching someone else is a wonderful way to reinforce learning, and it builds confidence in the older child. Many people have said to me, "Eight kids! How does your mother do it? I can't even handle my two." These commentators often do not realize that older children can take over many of the mother's responsibilities. A successful homeschool parent who teaches multiple grades is someone who has learned to be a good delegator. However, I have also seen parents take advantage of loyal older children, who end up shouldering too much of the responsibility.

As students get older, they should be learning to study and learn independently, but they still need careful evaluation by their homeschool teacher. Older students in a multilevel-teaching situation also need private time to study. They need a place to work that will be quiet and off-limits to younger children for several hours of the day. This seems obvious, but siblings have a way of sniffing out peaceful places and filling them with noise! It is very frustrating for middle or high school students if they do not have a time and place set aside for quiet study. Independent study habits formed in homeschool prepare students for college. When I entered college I was amazed by the terrible study habits of my classmates. Some of them simply had no idea of how to begin studying other than by reading the assigned material—if they could even get through that! They apparently had never heard of rereading, outlining, or rewriting their notes. In our homeschool Mom made us write book reports, research papers, stories, and poetry, most of the time requiring that they be typed and neatly presented, sometimes with artwork. I recommend that homeschool teachers require this caliber of work from their students. This is the type of work that prepared me for college. These homeschool projects gave me the boost I needed to get college scholarships and graduate debt free, without having to work full-time while in school.

My mother continually evaluates herself. While I was in

college she would ask me every now and then what skills or subjects would have better prepared me for college or life, and how she could improve the schooling of my siblings. A few days later I would hear one of my sisters grumble, "Where did Mom get the idea we that need more geography?" Mom's continual self-evaluation allows her to improve her teaching methods constantly. As a result, I suppose little Darleen will be the smartest of us all! I am not sure what that says about me. ☐

6

From Diapers to Diplomas

Danielle

I feel confident that my education at home has prepared me for college and life. I entered college as a sixteen-year-old, although I did not attend full-time the first year. Fall semester I took an open English course, in which we watched videos, read the books, and took a test at the college every month. In the spring semester I joined chorus and took voice lessons and a scuba-diving class. I had started music studies without jumping fully into college. At such a young age it was a good way to begin. The next year I took a full load and received a full scholarship. I believe I was well equipped spiritually to handle the ungodly influences all around me. Entering an arts program, my eyes were wide open in disbelief. Everything that I had heard about artists (including musicians) was true. Drugs, promiscuity, new-age philosophy, bad language, and wild living were normal for them. I learned to be accepting and loving without thinking their behavior normal. Not wanting a reputation as naive, I also learned to mask my shock! In the spring of the second year, the Lord answered my prayer for Christian friends. I became involved in InterVarsity Christian Fellowship, and became president of our chapter the following year.

The Lord has graciously directed and provided for my education from the beginning. I was able to transfer to Palm Beach Atlantic College, a private Christian college, on scholarships. I taught music for a semester at a Christian school while I continued to take music composition lessons. I am now attending law school. This past year has been exhausting, but they say that the first year of law school is the most difficult. I hope so. The study habits I developed in homeschool and continued in college have allowed me to survive law school and stay in the top 20% of my class and make the dean's list.

The promotion of postmodern thought in the classroom stunned me. It was very difficult to sit back and hear that truth no longer exists. I still have not figured out where they think it went! The law is not as helpful or as black and white as I had previously thought. But I know I have been called to law school for a reason, and I hope to defend homeschooling against legal attacks, if nothing else. The research skills my mother stressed have come in handy and helped make me a candidate for law review.

The Lord has used the opportunities I had in homeschool to develop teaching skills. One of the best opportunities I had was when my mother was using the Konos curriculum and co-oping with another family. I was four years older than the oldest child in the group, so they allowed me to teach a unit study every month. It was a great learning experience. They allowed me to experiment—some things worked and others did not. Where else could you gain that type of experience in such an environment? Only in homeschool.

When we chose the GED as our graduation option, it took care of much of the record keeping that is normally needed. The GED comes with its own transcript, so there is no need for homeschoolers to provide their own for colleges to review. Subjects, credits, and grade-point averages are all taken care of under the GED as far as colleges are concerned. The GED diploma has carried a certain stigma in the past because of its association with high school dropouts; but the reputation is unfair, and most people now realize that. All colleges accept the GED, though acceptable scores vary from school to school.

Upon entering college, I took the College Placement Test (CPT). I did not take the SAT because it was not necessary for admission to the community college. The CPT can be taken repeatedly, so my mother has often recommended that homeschoolers go to their community college, take the CPT, and see if they are ready for college. She calls me her little guinea pig, because she sent me to college at sixteen. She kept my sister home through all twelve grades and will keep the rest of the kids home through twelfth grade, too.

To apply for scholarships I made an appointment with the financial-aid officer at the college I planned to attend. The first step is to fill out the FAFSA form (for federal aid), since all other awards and financial aid are based upon that formula. In most cases this automatically applies you for state aid as well. If you demonstrate financial need based on your parents' income (unless you are independent), you may be awarded a Pell Grant. The amount of the award varies according to need. To fill out the FAFSA you will need the parents' and the student's W-2 forms and 1040 tax return form, or its equivalent. Filling it out for the first time is a little overwhelming, but the directions are very thorough.

Next, fill out the financial aid forms for the school you are attending. Do not neglect to do this. Thousands of dollars in scholarships remain unclaimed every year. Talent scholarships for music and theater are usually smaller in amount and usually require an audition. For these scholarships, contact the department you are interested in and schedule an audition. Your school's financial-aid officer should make you aware of any special requirements or forms for private scholarships. These are abundant at private schools.

Financial aid is out there, and everyone who truly needs it can get some. It is mostly a matter of talking to the financial-aid office, making your need known, and taking the time to fill out a stack of paperwork!

Graduating from homeschool has in no way hindered my social skills. In fact, I believe being homeschooled has accounted for my ability to withstand peer pressure from the college environment. It was actually very difficult for me in my first year at a Christian college because I was expecting the atmosphere to be drastically different from the public college. When I arrived, I found the same types of things going on, just not openly. My mother had tried to warn me, but still I was disappointed. Now as I look back, I see that there was more of a difference than I gave the school credit for; only a few people were living a worldly lifestyle, but they soured my taste for the whole student body. As I am applying to public graduate schools, I must confess, I do not look forward to going to a public college after attending a Christian college for two and a half years. However, I am completely ready and able to cope with the change in atmosphere, because of my previous experience at the community college. I am very thankful that I attended the public and not the Christian college first; otherwise I would not have been able to appreciate the Christian atmosphere (that costs so much extra money). The Lord's timing is always perfect. I look back amazed at how every piece fell into place. A unit study on rocks and minerals in our homeschool whetted my appetite for the geology course I took in college, which was the course in which I probably learned the most. It prompted a discussion on creation versus evolution in which my evolution-teaching professor brought his class to an InterVarsity-sponsored creation seminar!

Homeschooling might seem too difficult, or even impossible for you; it may not even seem like a good idea, but the Lord says in Isaiah 55:8, "For my thoughts are not your thoughts, neither are your ways my ways." God can do what seems impossible for us to do on our own. There is no better way to give him glory, which is our purpose here on earth, than by following his prompting. Our family has testified throughout this book that all of our success is from God. To God be the glory for the wonderful school years I spent at home being taught by my parents!   □

Donna

By being homeschooled, I am able to talk freely and openly with my parents about what I believe, or I can ask questions and know they are not being forced into silence by a system which has turned its face away from God. They can see how I have grown and am growing. I am growing spiritually because they are not only my teachers—they are my parents. We study and memorize the Scriptures together daily. Bible memorization is a regular part of our daily education.

I feel more confident and prepared to enter college because I have already been taught to study independently. I learned how to make my own decisions, not just follow the crowd. College would not be the "big adjustment" everyone tends to think if students already knew how to study independently. I met a few students who graduated the same year I did, a couple of them from a very elite private school. One afternoon our teacher told us to study the last few chapters alone because we did not have time to go over them in class. She then announced we would be tested on these chapters. After class as we discussed the situation, I felt the same anxiety I always feel before a test. I thought that I might need to get some help, but it was really not that big a deal. The other students, however, were really upset that she would dare test us on material we had not discussed in class. One or two even decided they would not show up on test day. Is that how public high school prepared them for college? I think in a conventional high school everything tends to be very laid out for the student. By the time students get to college some of them are not sure what to do, because they don't have anyone asking why they did not turn in an assignment or come to class; they just get marked down automatically or kicked out. Since I was in a lot of different social activities, there was no social adjustment for me. I even introduced myself to students who later told me I was the first person who talked to them. I also got along with my teachers, and I was able to communicate effectively with the teachers that were far from being my favorites. The biggest adjustment for me was finding my way around the huge campus! So if one of your reasons for not homeschooling through high school is the adjustment into college, scratch that off your list. It only took me a few days to figure out where all my classes were. If anything, the adjustment is easier for a homeschooler.   □

My intent in writing this book is to acknowledge God and share how he has led this family in our homeschool. So far I have painted a cozy picture of children, family, and the blessings of following Christ, but going down this narrow road is not always easy. Sometimes you feel all alone and the whole world seems to be against your convictions. In sharing how we have seen his fingerprints all over our lives and the lives of our children since we have taken on the task of their education, we hope to encourage those who are being called to school their children at home, especially those called to homeschool all the way through high school. Our objective is to give glory to the God of this family. We hope to show where, in areas of our inadequacy, God has adequately supplied all our needs.

Homeschooling the children God has loaned to us has been the greatest spiritual investment of our lives. With any investment come ups and downs. We have found that, most importantly, each day you must acknowledge God and show him he comes first in your lives by praying together, opening and reading his word together, and trying to live the righteous life that he desires.

Just the other day we took a shopping trip to the mall. Two of my children were not with me, as one was at college and the other on a trip with her grandmother. As we walked into a store in an orderly fashion, some people smiled and some sneered. Seeing a large family brings out many reactions. These reactions seem to characterize the mind-set of society today. I could write a book on the reactions and comments I have received about having such a large family. Some people are pleasant, some hateful, some encouraging, some critical. Often they do not intend to be critical, but feel they need to give advice when they see so many children. Others share stories about raising their own children. As you look at people in homes, malls, even churches, and observe their lives and listen to what they say, you can see how they are reflecting the moral standards of our society. When I look at movies, television, or radio, I begin to realize where all these comments and ideas materialize. I see the problems children face in the public schools, and even in private and Christian schools, and it does not take long to figure out where children learn this behavior. This behavior is an unspoken statement of where the hearts of the people are today.

One question commonly asked of my husband and me is, "Why would you keep your children at home, instead of sending them to school?" Working part-time within the public school system has enabled me to visit nine elementary schools and two middle schools almost daily. What I see and hear at these schools provides enough incentive to keep me on the road God has led me until I have completed the education of my youngest child. On my job I often have to substitute for crossing guards who are sick or cannot make their post. It seems I always end up at one particular school. I have privately nicknamed this school "Gates of Hell Elementary." I pray for these children. The guard who usually takes this post is also a Christian and shares with me how prayer for the children she meets has changed them.

One morning in early October I had seen the most glorious sunrise at the corner of the school. As the first student arrived, she greeted me with a pleasant "Hello." The day was going great so far. I had finished my morning prayers, witnessed God's handiwork in a sunrise, and been pleasantly greeted. I thought, *This school isn't so bad*. Now the sun was fully up and a group of middle school students were approaching the crosswalk to wait for the bus which picks them up at this elementary school. Middle school students sometimes think they are too old to bother with a crossing guard. Since this corner has heavy traffic, I always cross every student that approaches the crosswalk, middle or elementary. Instead of greeting one another pleasantly, I heard the students greet one another with language I would not repeat. One word in particular seems popular with this age group. I cringe when I hear it.

This school is located in a somewhat pleasant neighborhood populated by a diverse group of people. We have many cultures within the Ft. Lauderdale/Miami area. One girl, a real beauty, greeted me with smile as she crossed the street to join the larger group. I could not believe her dress. It did not look like a middle school girl's typical dress, but rather something which might be worn at a nightclub by a mature woman. As she greeted the group of kids, it was obvious that she was a leader. As the young men gathered around her, one boy complimented the tight dress. This fellow appeared to be twelve or thirteen years old. He began touching her above the waist while making comments about the action he was taking. She did not stop his admiration or his touching but just giggled rather playfully. The rest of the group laughed as they enjoyed the scene.

At the same time, a few yards away, another girl dressed very much like a boy leaned over the sidewalk and began to vomit. I was already quite shaken about the other girl, and now I felt bad for this sick little girl waiting for the bus. But when she saw the alarm on my face, she straightened up and began a loud, obnoxious, almost unnatural, laugh. She was not ill at all—she was just playing a joke to get attention. She wanted to impress the group and had succeeded in her task. After that morning session I reported all of this to my supervisor in hopes that this bus stop could be changed to a different location. The middle schoolers were constantly intimidating the younger students as they waited to go across the street to the elementary school.

Another incident had happened on this very corner one month earlier. It was in the afternoon when a large group of elementary school children approached the crossing. As I saw a gap in traffic and went into the street to cross the children, I reminded them to look both ways before crossing. This procedure helps them to develop traffic safety habits. All the children were safely across the street, except for one. He told me he would not leave the street and that no one could make him. By now the drivers who were waiting to proceed were getting impatient. I asked him again to get out of the road, and he answered no. Suddenly he pulled a large metal pipe from behind his back. He began swinging the pipe back and forth and dared me to make him cross. Cars were now honking, and traffic was driving around him. I asked two safety patrols standing nearby to alert a teacher I could see in the distance. Within a short time there were two teachers at the corner pleading with the boy to get out of the road. The young man swore at the teachers and told them they could not make him do anything.

I overheard the female teacher say to the male teacher, "Go across the street and pick up that pipe the boy has dropped."

The man replied, "I don't want to get shot."

That made me wonder if the boy had a reputation for being violent. He obviously did. What a shame to think that an elementary school child might carry a gun. The teachers were scared of him, even though he did not appear to have a gun. The young man eventually grew tired of the defiance and went home.

Things have changed since I was in school! Corporal punishment has been replaced with detentions and time-outs. I am thankful that by homeschooling I am able to deal with any discipline problems that may arise. And I am thankful that God is loving and gracious and does not deal with us in the way we deserve. If our children have broken a rule, we must follow the Scriptures and discipline them. We desire to train up our children in the way they should go. Deuteronomy 6:7 says of God's commandments, "Impress them on your children. Talk about them when you sit at home and when you walk along the road, when you lie down and when you get up." Isn't this a picture of a homeschool? Shouldn't this be the example we use? Deuteronomy 6:8 goes on to say, "Tie them as symbols on your hands and bind them on your foreheads." I am thankful that as homeschoolers we are able to teach the laws of God as well as his mercy and grace. As stewards of what God trusts us with, homeschool is a means by which we can teach such things to our children. We do not feel we would be doing right if we sent our children to public schools where, unfortunately, the dominant subjects appear to be peer pressure, dependency, humanism, worldly living, and evolution taught as fact rather than theory, where violence, drugs, and immorality replace prudence and integrity.

Over twenty-three years ago, far from home and family in Rochester, New York, where my husband was attending college, our first child was born. After her birth, unsurpassed joy was what I felt as I looked into the face that God had created and entrusted to us. It was then that I felt a great burden for her training. I knew at that moment many years of prayer, discipline, and soul searching must be done to honor the giver and maker of such a wonderful baby. Since then seven other wonders of his handiwork have been loaned to us. Considering the potential of each child and the awesomeness of having such a powerful influence on their lives makes us aware of our responsibilities. As we considered our oldest's training and what was available as far as schools, we searched the Scriptures. I remembered what Romans 16:17 says, "I urge you, brothers, to watch out for those who cause divisions and put obstacles in your way that are contrary to the teaching you have learned. Keep away from them." Children are so impressionable—should not all their educational topics be taught in the light of God's Word? Is it not the character attributes we teach, rather than the knowledge we impart, that is most important?

I have heard some argue that they want their children to go to public school as missionaries. I do not wish to disagree with such a case if God has called them to that, but I do warn people who tell me this to be careful when sending innocent children into a system that is full of trained teachers, some of whom are staunch believers in the system they represent. I pray daily for the children in the public-school system, both those who are Christian and those who are not.

People have a variety of reasons to homeschool their children. Being on the steering committee for our home-school support group, I receive phone calls from people who have started a homeschool program or plan to. Some want to homeschool for a few months to straighten out a problem with their child, some want to homeschool for a year, and some plan to homeschool up until high school. I remind them that many children today cannot make it in public high school due to absences, fighting, drugs, or gangs. I ask them if they want their children in this type of environment.

When I started homeschooling Donielle in sixth grade, I knew I would teach her all the way through high school. It was a step of faith for me. Where I have lacked, God has accommodated. If you have been called to homeschool your children, to take on the responsibility of their education, such a task cannot be taken halfheartedly. If we are called and take the call and the responsibility seriously, the Lord will surely provide all our needs. Whatever hardships arise, if we put it all in his hands, he will carry us through. When we toil in the tasks God has given us, we must concentrate on our families. Such an investment can change and influence both our nation and the world. We must have the right focus and concentrate on the principles of God's Word. Such a diligent investment in homeschooling our children will not be in vain.

What are the fundamentals of a good homeschool? First of all, the salvation of our own children. Seeing each of our children put their complete faith in Jesus Christ should be our goal. Such a goal can be blessed in an abundant way. If we take the opportunity to school our children in prayer, according to God's Word, we can relate to Psalm 92:12-13, "The righteous will flourish like a palm tree, they will grow like a cedar of Lebanon; planted in the house of the Lord, they will flourish in the courts of our God." Your children will rise up and call you blessed!

Another fundamental of a good homeschool is realizing that we are stewards of that with which God has entrusted us. When our children were born we ceremoniously gave them back to him. "All that we have is thine alone, a trust, O Lord, from thee," we told the Lord. "They are yours; direct us to care for them, and use us to raise each one for your glory."

A friend of ours was recently talking about his children. When I complemented him on his daughter's sweet spirit and good behavior, he replied, "It's not anything I did, she is God's child." I don't think he realized her good behavior did not just happen, but rather was the result of his and his wife's diligence to rear her in the light of God's Word. There are so many factors involved in raising good children. I do not in any way claim to be an expert. I always know that all I can do is follow in the way my Savior leads me. Realizing that my children are the Lord's helps us to do our best in raising them. Not a day goes by that I am not thankful we made the decision to homeschool. Now that two are grown, we see the fruits of our labors. Whatever hardships arose along the way, we do not regret their godly education. We are thankful for the closeness we have with them, and we are especially thankful that we homeschooled them all the way through high school. Looking at the uniqueness of each of our children, I can think of no other way than to go through high school with each. If someone offered me scholarships to the very best of Christian or private schools for all of the children, I would answer, "No, thank you, their education is our responsibility." When God's will was revealed to us and we obeyed him, he left the fingerprints of his hands on our lives every day and in every way. He has met every one of our children's needs, both spiritually and physically.

If God is calling you, if he is leading you down this road, if he is speaking to your heart, listen to him. Do not drown out his still, small voice with excuses. Do not be blinded by what the world is telling you is best for your children. Do not be fooled into believing that you have to send your children to a "school" for their education. What we grew up with or what seems to be right, may be a hindrance to submitting to God's vision for the lives of our children. We could list a million excuses for why we should not homeschool. This list is written by the world. It does not take a village to raise a child. It takes a mom and dad with a solid faith in Christ and a desire for their children to have the same faith. You will be able to share in the same blessings I have described throughout this book and see his fingerprints in your life and the lives of your children if you are called to this mission. I believe there are many Christian parents called to school their children at home, all the way through high school. If God is calling you, accept his challenge. He will provide and he will be glorified.

Have you caught the vision of what homeschooling really is? Do you have a quiver full of blessings God has entrusted to you for nurturing? Are these children arrows in the hands of you, the warrior? Are you the one responsible for training them to defeat the enemy in all his tactics? Are your children able to distinguish between good and evil? You are in control of your own home. You make the rules, you decide where it is located, how it looks inside. Are you pleased? Is your home a haven for drug abuse, bad language, bad music, illicit sex, violence, metal detectors, guns, and homosexuality? Do you need an officer of the law to patrol your lawn? What are you building inside those four walls of your home? On the walls of your classroom do you display the laws of God? Can your children openly talk about sin and the redemption purchased by Christ? During the school day are you with them, teaching character and the principles of God's Word, or are you sending them off to strangers to be taught in a system that is contrary to the foundations of our Christian faith? You may say that you send your children to a Christian school, and that these things do not go on there! These worldly attitudes and the foolishness of the mind can go on even in the Christian schools. I Peter 4:17 says, "For it is time for judgment to begin with the family of God." Are you willing for others to do the job God has called you to do? The Word of God should be the foundation of all subject matter taught in school. The lordship of Christ should reign paramount over all areas of the schools. I like to reflect on the words of King David in I Chronicles 17:16, "Who am I, O Lord God, and what is my family, that you have brought me this far?" We have caught this vision. We have yielded to God's call to take control. We have seen the results, by his grace.

Do you want to homeschool, or do you want to put a school into your home? If by reading this book you have caught a vision of what homeschool really is, then I pray you will acknowledge him in all your ways and watch him direct your path in the lives of your children. He will become the administrator of your homeschool, diapers to diploma. Your children will be blessed with an education that can not be matched at the best of schools.

Valuable Resources for Homeschoolers

The Simplicity of Homeschooling: Discover the Freedom of Learning Through Living
By Vicky Goodchild, 800-377-0390

This book is beneficial to those contemplating home-schooling as well as the veteran and everyone in between! It encourages a style of educating that promises freedom, simplicity, and joy in learning through living. Homeschool-ing is presented as a lifestyle rather than a system of educa-tion. The author helps develop a "learning lifestyle" that is unique to your family. Also available is an audiotape, *A Father's Perspective,* by Vicky's husband, Jack.

The Complete Guide to Successful Co-oping
By Linda Koeser and Lori Marse, 13341 Barwick Road, Delray Beach, FL 33445, 561-498-0672

This book describes the experiences of two successful homeschooling moms whose favorite and most productive homeschool years were those in which they co-oped. Linda and Lori have included countless ideas, examples of log sheets, and a complete unit study.

4-H Clubs County Agriculture and Extension Services

4-H can be an integral part of homeschooling, offering the leadership, citizenship, and public speaking skills needed in a child's future. This is a parent-child organization with lots of hands-on involvement. Topics range from animal science and rocketry to nutrition and bicycle safety. There are scholarship opportunities for those in high school and many competitions. Look for your local Agricultural Extension Office and start your own club of other homeschoolers or neighborhood children.

A Beka Books

P.O. Box 19100, Pensacola, FL 32523-9160, 800-874-2352, www.abeka.com

This is an excellent curriculum from a Christian perspective for all grade levels. Donielle especially enjoyed their science and literature textbooks. The readers are recommended for young children, and the video course for high school students is a good, rigorously structured college preparation.

Affordable Christian Textbooks and Supplies

262 Hawthorne Village Commons Suite 321, Vernon Hills, IL 60061, 800-889-2287

This is a supply catalog with a little bit of everything at good prices.

Alpha and Omega Publications

33 N. McKemy Avenue, Chandler, AZ 85226, 800-682-7391

Alpha and Omega has complete curricula for grades

1–12. Before starting the program, you can use their test for proper placement. It is helpful in locating weak areas that need to be reinforced or concepts that have been missed. Each subject is presented in ten workbooks, full of interesting examples and colorful illustrations. The lightweight books are convenient for those on the go. The teacher's manuals include reduced sample pages from the student's books complete with answers and instructions. Alpha and Omega is very manageable and interesting. Almost no planning is needed as every subject is laid out, detailing what will be covered in each book. Each subject broken up into ten Lifepacs, allowing children to catch up in weak areas.

Backyard Scientist
P.O. Box 16966, Irvine, CA 92713, 714-551-2392

Jane Hoffman leads you through experiments using items that are found in the home. The hands-on discovery method takes children from concept through observation and performance of each experiment. Conclusions are then based on the evidence.

Bob Jones University Press
Greenville, SC 29614, 800-845-5731

Originally started to supply classroom materials to Christian schools, their foundation is built on biblical philosophical principles of education. They believe that education is not Christian unless "transformation through the renewing of the mind" through the power of the Holy Spirit is evident in the fabric of the curriculum and the teaching and learning. Their quality material contains activity-oriented unit themes, appealing graphics, and high-interest content with emphasis on thinking skills. Curricula are available for grades pre-K through twelve. They also reach out to homeschool families by conducting an annual Home Education Leadership Program every summer, with activities for each family member.

Calvert School
105 Tuscany Road, Baltimore, MD 21210, 410-243-6030, e-mail: inquiry@calvertschool.org

This curriculum is based on a Judeo-Christian viewpoint. It is a classic approach using textbooks in each subject with heavy emphasis on reading and writing. The strong use of creative writing is much appreciated. They also offer subjects such as architecture, art and music. Their *Child's History of the World* is probably the finest children's history book in print.

Censored Science
P.O. Box 457, Morriston, FL 32668, 352-528-2255, censoredsci@mfi.net

The mission of this nonprofit ministry is to glorify God and further the gospel by "destroying speculations and every lofty thing raised up against the knowledge of God"(2 Corinthians 10:5 NASB). They offer the often-censored scientific evidence that confirms the biblical account of origins and history by teaching the Biblical Scientific Creation Models of Origins in an entertaining, chronological and friendly way. By effectively answering common questions, this scientific scenario enables people to translate secular interpretations into a biblical framework, giving them the confidence, encouragement and freedom that comes from knowing that God's Word is true.

Christian Liberty Academy Satellite Schools

502 W. Euclid Avenue, Arlington Heights, IL 60002,
847-259-8736

We call this school-at-home, as opposed to home-schooling. CLA is convenient because they offer a preliminary placement test. Unit tests are mailed to your "teacher" who grades them. The structured program works well for those lacking confidence in their teaching ability, or for those who work and have less time for teaching.

Creation Studies Institute

5620 N.E. 22 Avenue, Ft. Lauderdale, FL 33308,
954-771-1652 or 800-882-0278, CSINFO.org

This is a nonprofit organization, training laypeople and children with the truth about evolution's myths using facts of geochronometers and good science to support God's Word. They offer workshops to homeschool families using lab experiments (such as making rockets that blast off!). They host seminars with Creation Science speakers and have a weekly radio call-in program, The Genesis Connection, which is simulcast on the Internet via WAFG.com. Join a Fossil Float each spring and fall in Arcadia, FL, to find fossils (which you may keep).

Dorling Kindersley Family Learning

Amala & Ian Narod, Authorized Independent Certified
School Sales Distributors, 954-252-1388,
E-mail: ParadiseSchool@hotmail.com

Their mission is to create home learning centers which offer award-winning DK books, CDs and nature videos, as seen on public television and Disney, with photography that leads off the page (or screen)! They are the creators of the *Eyewitness Books*.

Five in a Row Publishing
14901 Pineview Drive, Grandview, MO 64030-4509, 816-331-5769

Written by Jane Claire Lambert, this is a literature-based, unit-study curriculum geared for four- to eight-year-olds. The "texts" are the excellent children's books which can be found in the public library. One book is read to the children each day, five days in a row. Each day a different subject is discussed in relation to the story, either art, social studies, math, science, or language arts. It's amazing how many lessons can be taught from one book! Children never got bored reading the same book. On the contrary, they continue to ask for the stories long after the unit is finished! You do not have to spend a lot of time in preparation, but you do spend a lot of time with your child as you snuggle and read together. This time spent is priceless.

Geography Matters
800-426-4650, www.geomatters.com,
e-mail: Geomatters@earthlink.net

They specialize in geography resources, especially outline maps. They carry geography, history, and science curricula for grades K–12. The *Ultimate Geography and Timeline Guide* is one you will use year after year. It includes maps, lesson plans and 340 reproducible timelines. *The Scientist's Apprentice* is a science curriculum that you can use with all of your elementary children simultaneously. Experiments, games, crafts, songs, and recipes appeal to different learning styles and make science fun.

God's World Publications

P.O. Box 2330, Asheville, NC 28802, 704-253-8063 or 800-951-KIDS

Donna enjoyed *God's World* from first through sixth grade. This is a weekly newspaper for pre-K–12, with different papers for each grade. An animal mascot guides the child through each issue with word-search or crossword puzzles, helping the child review what they have read. Each issue includes a teacher's guide.

Home School Legal Defense Association

P.O. Box 3000, Purcellville, VA 20134, 540-338-5600, www.hslda.org

This national nonprofit organization was established expressly for the purpose of defending the rights of parents who choose to homeschool their children. Each year they handle thousands of cases for member families who are challenged legally in the area of homeschooling. They have been a barrier, stopping legal attempts to infringe on freedoms of homeschoolers. They serve as a clearinghouse for research, news, and resources. Members of their legal team speak at homeschool conferences around the country. Membership is $100 per family, per year. Membership guarantees representation and counsel by qualified attorneys familiar with homeschooling issues. Also included are publications and periodicals as well as the opportunity to invest in protecting homeschooling.

John Holt's Bookstore

2269 Massachusetts Avenue, Cambridge, MD 02140-1226, 617-864-3100

John Holt offers passionate and creative views on education through his book *How Schools Fail*. His newsletter, *Growing Without Schooling,* gives wonderful ideas for problem solving and lets you peek into other homes and see how they creatively direct their children's education. He provides suggestions on how to get school credits, degrees, diplomas, other publications, and educational catalogs. He offers a wide range of opinions and ideas useful throughout the homeschool experience.

KONOS Curriculum

P.O. Box 1534, Richardson, TX 75083, 214-669-8337

KONOS is a hands-on, unit study, discovery learning curriculum. With KONOS children *do,* not just read of how anything is or was done. They role-play characters in history, while learning godly character by good examples. It can be adapted for any grade up to seventh, with units clustered under character traits. There are special guidelines for high schoolers to be self-taught. This is a good curriculum for high schoolers to help teach. This is not a fill-in-the-blank curriculum! It is active and messy! Get the KONOS *Compass* to see how scope and sequence works.

Lifetime Books and Gifts

3900 Chalet Suzanne Drive, Lake Wales, FL 33853, 941-676-6311

Lifetime is more than a catalog: *Lifetime* carries books from the foundations of homeschooling to math, language, classic book selections, science, and every conceivable subject in between. The Farewells are homeschoolers who offer a service to homeschoolers with what they carry and with the helpful hints in the catalog.

Math-U-See
5050 Ocean Beach Blvd. #104, Cocoa Beach, FL 32931, 800-434-0007 or 888-854-MATH

This is a comprehensive math curriculum that provides a foundation, building "precept upon precept." Manipulatives are used to teach new concepts. If you find math easy to understand but difficult to explain, the teaching manuals and videos provide the knowledge to facilitate the instruction of concepts. The curriculum is presented in a systematic and sequential format, making the learning of new concepts a logical progression from previously mastered material.

Memlok Bible Memory System
420 East Montwood Avenue, LaHabra, CA 90631-7411, 800-373-1947

Donna explains Memlok: We use Memlok every night to memorize Scripture. On the front of each card is a picture associated with a Bible verse. By looking at the picture and saying the Bible verse each day, it locks the verse in your memory.

Rod and Staff Publications
412 Cheesebrew Lane Thurman, OH 45685, 740-245-5358

Using Rod and Staff readers and accompanying phonics workbooks provides a strong foundation for children. Not only are they thorough in their approach to teaching a child to read, but they are pleasantly wholesome in content. Children enjoy coloring and painting the simple pen and ink drawings found in the workbooks. It is a joy and time-saver to teach reading, writing, phonics, truth, and character to children simultaneously, while enjoying discussions, prompted by the material that serves to shape and influence our lives forever!

Sing, Spell, Read and Write
1000 112 Circle N. #100, St. Petersburg, FL 33716, 800-321-8322

Children first learn simple songs that teach the sounds of letters and then proceed to the short vowels in song. Later long vowels and blends are learned with the help of catchy tunes. Children write, learn spelling, and read books designed for success.

Sonlight Curriculum
8121 S. Grant Way, Littleton, CO 80122, 303-730-6292

Sonlight spotlights history as their centerpiece. They choose all the literature that the children read from a given time period. Their spelling program is strong phonetically, their literature is classic, and their history is compelling.

Usborne Books
1264 Alhambra Drive, Ft. Myers, FL 33901, 941-332-7138

Usborne books is an excellent resource for science and social studies. If you want to have a book party this is the one. Invite all your homeschooling friends, and the books sell themselves. They are unique, full of information, colorful, and organized in a child-friendly format. These are the kind of books kids pick up in their spare time and read for fun!

Helpful Homeschool Web sites

http://christianbooks.com
Christian books from many publishers on all topics are available here.

www.home-ed-press.com
This Web site is sponsored by *Home Education Magazine,* and is full of resources and good ideas.

http://homeschooling.faithweb.com
This is a place where you can get questions answered and link to other sites.

www.letstalkabout.com
This is a "support group" for homeschoolers which includes interesting articles.